Everything I've Ever
Done That Worked

Please visit Hay House UK: www.hayhouse.co.uk;
Hay House USA: www.hayhouse.com;
Hay House Australia: www.hayhouse.com.au;
Hay House South Africa: www.hayhouse.co.za

Everything I've Ever Done That Worked

Lesley Garner

HAY HOUSE

Australia • Canada • Hong Kong
South Africa • United Kingdom • United States

Reprinted 2008, 2009

First Published in the United Kingdom 2004
Hay House UK, Ltd. 292B Kensal Road, London W10 5BE
Phone: 44-20-8962-1230 Fax: 44-20-8962-1239 www.hayhouse.co.uk

First published in Australia 2004
Hay House Australia, Ltd., 18/36 Ralph Street, Alexandria NSW 2015
Phone: 612-9669-4299 Fax: 612-9669-4144 www.hayhouse.com.au

First published in the United States 2005
Hay House, Inc., P.O. Box 5100, Carlsbad, CA 92018-5100
Phone: 1-760 431-7695 or 1-800 654-5126
Fax: 1-760 431-6948 or 1-800 650-5115 (fax) www.hayhouse.com

Cover design by Leanne Siu
Interior design by e-Digital
Edited by Lizzie Hutchins

08 07 06 05 04   5 4 3 2 1
1st printing May 2006
A CIP catalogue record for this book is available from the British Library

ISBN-10 1-4019-1106-4 (paperback)
ISBN-13 978-1-4019-1106-5 (paperback)

ISBN-10 1-4019-0340-1 (hardback)
ISBN-13 978-1-4019-0340-4 (hardback)

Typeset by e-Digital
Printed and bound in Great Britain by TJ International, Padstow, Cornwall.

Praise for

Everything I've Ever Done That Worked

'This book is a huge celebration of life and how we can in simple ways enrich our days ... I recommend it to anyone who wants to feel happier, more fulfilled and increasingly to enjoy the world around them.'
Jilly Cooper

'A priceless collection of reflections, observations and signposts towards a happier and more harmonious life. Wise, practical, elegant, inspiring and genuinely helpful.'
Mick Brown, author of *The Spiritual Tourist*

'Lesley Garner is one of those remarkable women who is original, full of insights and common sense, while writing with a sparkle and fluency that is envied by her peers and hugely enjoyed by her many admirers.'
Sir Max Hastings – former Editor of the *Daily Telegraph* and the *Evening Standard*

Contents

Acknowledgements

This is both my acknowledgement of my debt of gratitude and my dedication of this book to those who have helped and accompanied me.

This little book represents the distillation of years of my own efforts to get a grip on both happiness and the meaning of life. Luckily for me, there was always good company along the way. Some people have been there for the long haul, others simply shared a part of the journey. Some just said or did the thing that made all the difference at the time. Some were fellow students, some valued teachers, and of course it is quite possible to be both at once.

The following people have given me friendship, support, teaching, common sense, encouragement, direction, humour, wisdom and invaluable companionship. Thank you very much indeed to Marianna Alexander, Gay Baynes, Leonard Bernstein, David Braybrook, Rosie and Eric Brown, Ben Cannon, Anne Dickson, Frances d'Souza, Peter Ford, Migs Goodman, Jo Ellen Grzyb, Fiona Harrold, Gloria Karpinski, Malcolm and Jane Lazarus, Gavin Maughling, Sheila Morley, Caroline Mustill, Carole Radford, Caroline Reynolds, Jenny Ridgewell, Veronica Roberts, Deidre, Rick and Susie Sanders, Mike Ward and to all my fellow participants on Gloria's Dakshina workshops in England, Germany, Scotland and Iceland: Anita, Detel, Dora, Hildur, Kolbrun, Liza, Sarah and Unnur.

In direct connection with this book I specially want to thank Mick Brown, Jilly Cooper and Max Hastings for their hugely appreciated encouragement and the team at Hay House – Jo Lal, Megan Slyfield and most particularly Michelle Pilley – for their responsiveness, care and professionalism.

And of course I want to thank my immediate family – my parents for their wisdom and example, and my two daughters, Harriet and Rachel, for their energy and their continual invaluable reminder that you can be happy, wise and optimistic without ever going on any courses at all.

Introduction

Some people have first aid boxes. Some people keep recipe books. Some people have tool kits. I keep a resource book – everything I've ever done that worked. In moments of confusion, indecision, panic, depression, stress and plain insomnia I can pick it up and know I'll find something in its pages that will dig me out and move me on.

There are things in here that work in darkness and things that work in daylight. There are techniques that will help you in planning your journey through life and techniques that will light the next inch of the path when you've lost your way, or even dig you out of the swamp into which you have fallen.

This isn't the single-answer approach. This isn't a guide to the one true Way. There are hundreds of ways and I have tried many of them. This is my personal greatest hits, my tested and recommended short cuts.

I am not a guru, a psychologist or a workshop leader. I am a journalist, a writer and someone who has followed many alleys out of personal need and curiosity. I have collected what is in these pages from workshops and journeys, professional experience and private crises, altered states and guided meditations, tribal wisdom and family lore, religious tradition and successful improvisation, and from the tried and tested experience of friends and teachers. But none of it is second hand because everything here has worked for me, personally, at some moment in my life.

My resource book represents a lifetime's searching and finding, and I think it is too good and too useful to keep to myself. I would love it to help other people too. I know as a writer that the best communication is when a reader says that what I wrote really helped or enlightened them. I hope this book will do that. I hope it will be a friend to other people.

Is it really everything I've ever done that worked? No. I don't tell you how to fix an electric plug or roast a chicken, though I can do those things too, and they work. I admit that knowing how to change a plug and roast a chicken are also life-enhancing, even life-saving, skills, but you can find household and cookery tips elsewhere. What I am interested in here is what you can do that can turn dark to light in the middle of a sleepless night, improve the quality of your relationships, help you decide on and follow a true course of action, rekindle enthusiasm and passion, give you fresh perspectives and new ideas and throw you a lifeline in the dark nights of the soul that come to everyone.

We begin coping with whatever life throws at us from the moment we are born, and we cope with it in a way that is partially determined by our inherent make-up, the gifts and characteristics already determined by our genes. The business of learning what works for you begins at once. One baby can cry and immediately be fed. Another, born into a time of famine or into a different family, can cry and never be fed. But for you, reading this book, life isn't so extreme. You have survived infancy, adolescence. You have made choices and maybe you are beginning to learn that what worked in one situation is a disadvantage in another.

You may have done all the things that worked up to now. You may have got the education, found a job, been through relationships, but you wouldn't have picked up this book if you weren't wondering whether there might be something more, something you've missed, something else that might make you happier, turn up the colour and volume of your life, give it narrative and meaning.

You're not alone. Since the Greeks of the fifth century BC, if not before, people have applied their minds to considering the meaning of life and our part in it. They have wondered how to behave in relation to everything that is larger than us –the gods, the universe. They have asked what it means to lead a good life. Our lives are immeasurably different from the lives of the ancient Greeks, but the fundamental questions and longings remain the same: how, in a time of danger and chaos, can an individual find meaning and fulfilment? And how, specifically, can I, with my personality, upbringing, tastes and talents, find a place in the world which satisfies me and relates me to the people who matter in my life?

So this book is partly philosophy and partly self-help. Self-help books sell in their millions and they are a very soft target for those who never read them. But the ancient Greeks were in the business of self-help as they argued about the good life on the hillsides of Athens. Where they differed from us today is that they used the tools of rigorous intellectual debate. They weren't in the business of providing emotional comfort, which is the territory of the self-help book.

Self-help books offer a refuge when your friends' patience or experience has run out. Self-help books offer comfort. Self-help books are friends. The danger is that they offer easy formulae, glib answers. They can encourage self-indulgence, sloppy thinking, clichéd thought. I hope I don't do that. I am not offering answers, only ways in which you might arrive at your own. This is why the emphasis is on what I've tried that works. I've kept an open mind. I've been eclectic. I haven't subscribed to one school of thought. I've tried to reconcile what I was taught through tradition with what I've worked out for myself.

And this book is partly memoir. The more I have written, the more I realize that it is a kind of autobiography. You will learn something about the life I've led, the places I've lived in and travelled to, the jobs I've done, what upsets me, what moves me, what thrills me. I am naturally a reflective and contemplative person and you might be very physical and active. Nevertheless, I might have had experiences that you might find helpful. The things in this book work for me because of who I am and the way I see the world. I am me, separate from you. But we are also both human. If we share 90 percent of our DNA with a mouse, I share a lot more than that with you, though you could be another race, another age, another sex.

Whenever I have a new experience I wonder how it could be useful, how I could relate it to other people. This is where being a writer comes in. I've been a journalist all my working life, which means that I am innately curious. I get to meet and question a lot of people, sometimes in extreme situations. I have been in presidential palaces and refugee camps. I have interviewed royalty, rape victims, millionaires, illegal immigrants, film stars, artists, politicians, musicians, sportsmen and women, children and the very old. I have learned from all of them and I love making the connections, picking up the experience and information that I can pass on.

Being a journalist also means I constantly have to justify myself to my peers – highly sceptical, critical people. As one former colleague famously said, his first reaction on interviewing any politician was to think, *Why is this bastard lying to me*? I'm not that cynical, but I'm trained not to be credulous either.

I am also a daughter, a mother, a friend. My life, like that of millions of women around the world, has been a constant micro-shifting balance between keeping myself, my employers and my family happy. I have spent years constantly monitoring this balance and being aware that somewhere at my centre is a still, true point. It is a point at which I am at rest but not inert. It is a point at which self-belief, energy, vision, enthusiasm and the capacity for happiness are renewed.

This point, which exists in all of us, is like a wellspring which is constantly under threat from pollution, weeds, other people's rubbish. It may be clogged, poisoned, dried up, built over. Some people aren't even aware that it exists. I wasn't even aware, until I started to write this paragraph, that this was how I saw it. We are our own source, our own wellspring. When I say 'everything I've ever done that worked', I mean 'everything I've ever done that worked to locate, maintain and protect my own wellspring'.

This is constant, vigilant labour and sometimes we need help. I have taken myself – my body, my intelligence, my heart, my spirit, my imagination – into all kinds of byways in search of more understanding and experience. I've taken part in workshops and rituals, retreats and processes. I've read books, undergone therapy. I've travelled. I've talked. I've cried, danced, sung, walked, explored, painted, talked with hundreds of others on the same search. Often I've thought, *If my friends could see me now.*

If I think I will learn something that will enlarge my experience of life, balance body and soul, heart and mind, and give me more understanding as a writer, more patience as a mother, more loving-kindness as a daughter, more sensitivity and perception as a listener and more creative energy as a writer, and if the people offering the something seem to have integrity, talent and skill, then I'll do it if the moment is right. The only path I have never trodden in pursuit of opening my doors of perception is that of drugs. I have learned to avoid experiences that give you hangovers or let-downs or which might permanently damage you. Besides, there are many more subtle and less dangerous ways to alter your state of consciousness and your view of the world than taking toxic substances. Some of them are in this book.

This is a circular book, by the way. You don't have to read it in any order. You can dip in and out as you please. I hope it will be of use and comfort to you, but only you know what your needs are. I would add to everything I have said here that there are times when self-help isn't enough, and this book is not a substitute for medical, therapeutic or professional help if you need it. In emergencies I recommend you turn to 'Emotional Freedom Technique', 'Fleeting Feelings', 'Calm Down', 'Practise Gratitude', 'Write a Letter to God' and 'The Magic of 20 Minutes'.

Be Glad You're Free

Let me tell you a story.

It's a story about a point in my life when I was without a regular job and in a great deal of confusion as to what I should do next. A 10-year relationship with a newspaper had come to an end, as these things do, and part of me wasn't at all sorry. I was burnt out. Only that summer I had been having dinner with an old friend who was also a journalist and we'd confessed over our glasses of wine that she wouldn't care if she never gave another piece of advice ever again and I wouldn't care if I never had another opinion.

But having opinions was what I did for a living and as the days went past I began to realize that I had been doing the same thing for too long to have any fresh ideas at all. I found myself approaching editors and saying that I would love to write for them, while a tired little voice in my head muttered, 'Oh no, you wouldn't.' I am sure that ambivalence communicates itself just as powerfully as enthusiasm and I wasn't surprised when these meetings failed to translate into jobs which I didn't really want anyway. So why was I wasting their time and mine? What else could I do?

One very beautiful morning in March, I got up and followed my routine. Make coffee. Scan the papers. Make notes of topics I could write on. Ring a couple of editors with suggestions and then wait for them to get back to me after morning conference. It was half past 10 and I knew nobody would get back to me before 12. *Blow it*, I thought. *I'm going out for a walk.*

I'm lucky enough to live near Richmond Park, an ancient deer forest and nature reserve on the edge of London, where herds of red and fallow deer graze freely and woodpeckers, owls, even a flock of green parakeets perch in ancient trees. In the woodland garden at the heart of the park I sat on a log and watched small birds building nests in the treetops while white spring clouds flew smartly overhead in the fresh wind. *Really*, I thought, *it's not so bad being out of work*. I thought of all my friends and colleagues stuck behind computers in grey airless offices while I breathed in the fresh scent of grass and watched tiny birds ferrying twigs overhead in the budding branches. Lucky me.

But I still needed an answer to my dilemma. *What on earth*, I thought, *should I be doing*? All I knew was that the way I was going about pursuing my career wasn't working.

I began to think about a book I'd bought in Paris a month earlier, *An Inquiry into the Existence of Guardian Angels*. I'd bought it because when I'd flicked through the pages I'd read that the author was a journalist who had had the extraordinary experience of being inexplicably saved from a sniper's bullet. He quoted other witnesses to acts of miraculous protection and timely guidance, many of them tough old reporters, foreign correspondents who had inexplicably been diverted from disaster, seasoned old cynics who nevertheless acknowledged an intervening mystery at some crucial moment in their life. I could relate to them and their experience and I was intrigued.

The author's argument was that guardian angels do exist. 'What is more,' he said, 'you can build a relationship with your guardian angel by creating a dialogue, preferably out loud. You'll find that angels will communicate and that they often have a strong sense of humour.' It was an interesting book but I hadn't thought about it until it came into my mind on my log in the wood.

There were no other people in sight on that spring morning and as I idly watched the clouds and the nest-building birds I found myself talking out loud. 'OK, guardian angel,' I said, 'if you exist, I'd like to know what on earth I should be doing about my career. Should I be looking for another column? A full-time job? A contract? With whom? Please give me a clue, and I'd like some sort of answer before I get back to the car park.'

I carried on sitting on my log. The birds carried on twittering and nest building. The little clouds carried on sailing over from the west. Nothing happened. Eventually I got up and carried on walking and I was so absorbed by the signs of spring all round me that I quite forgot about my request for an angelic message.

Half an hour later I had turned back towards the car park and I was crossing a wide open area of grassland when something caught my eye by the side of the path ahead. The plain where I was walking was deserted, nothing but grasses bending in the wind and little clumps of trees. Nobody else seemed to be out walking and I hadn't seen another person in the hour I'd been in the park.

What I found, planted in the grass at the edge of the path where no such thing had ever been or has been since, was a rough wooden stick with a square of brown cardboard stuck on the top of it. Written on the piece of cardboard were the misspelt words: 'B glad your free.'

Be glad you're free. I laughed and laughed out loud. I turned and looked round 360 degrees. Nobody. 'OK,' I said out loud. 'Thank you. I get it.' And I got it.

Those words changed everything. I was free. Why was I struggling to chain myself up again? When I got home I wrote them down in my diary, a daily reminder not to panic, not to do the conventional thing, not to try to walk back the way I'd come. *Be glad you're free.* The price of freedom is insecurity, but security is often an illusion. Each time I wobbled or got into a panic I remembered I was glad I was free.

Those words and the manner of their delivery stopped me in my tracks. They turned fear and negativity to hope and courage. They stopped me banging my head against a brick wall and encouraged me to take a deep breath and look around. With those words in mind I took advice that led me to decide not to do any work that didn't positively excite me. I went to art school and I began to write about art. By the time I found myself being a columnist again, which I did, I was renewed. I had different experience and perspective to bring to my writing.

I don't know if I'd had an angelic encounter or experienced a purely human coincidence. It doesn't matter. It had worked and it carries on working. The message is for you too. Be glad you're free. Because you are as free as you think you are.

Getting Started, Every Time

It is Tuesday morning. I'm already a day late. Why didn't I start on Monday? I am sitting at a table in my office and I am feeling besieged and overwhelmed. This is the morning I am determined to get into the daily rhythm of writing this book. This is the day I stop procrastinating.

I am feeling slightly sick. I am surrounded by piles of files and notes and feel that if I open my mouth to scream, a flock of papers will fly in and suffocate me. I know that I am feeling what thousands of people, millions of people, feel at the outset of a big project. I feel panic. I've got project paralysis. My thoughts are jeering at me from the branches of my mind like a flock of sassy black crows. *Think you can write a book? Everything I've Ever Done That Worked? Well, nothing's working now. Who are you? Thought it was easy when you had lunch with the publisher, didn't you? Thought it was clever when you wrote lots of headings down on a sheet of paper, didn't you?*

And what makes you so precious that you think you can retreat into your own world to do this? You do realize there's no food in the fridge and you've got to go down the supermarket? You know that the frame of your office window is rotting and you meant to call the carpenters two weeks ago. You know there's a pile of ironing waiting for you and that's why you can't find your blue shirt?

And if you're so determined to devote yourself to writing this book, why have you let this week's diary get so full? Check it out. You've got a dental appointment tomorrow, followed by an editorial board meeting, followed by a choir rehearsal. Won't get much writing done then. You've arranged to see your mortgage adviser the day after tomorrow and she needs an update on your financial situation which you haven't prepared. You meant to send flowers to that friend who drove you to hospital last week and you ought to ring your sick parents to see if their medical test results have come through…

Aaaaargh! That's the thing about having a head full of crows – they never shut up. And they have a wonderful vantage point. Your fears and insecurities are laid out below them like so much roadkill. There is only one way to deal with them. There is only one cure for procrastination. There is only one answer to the perennial fear of getting started, and that is to take an action, no matter how small, that will move you towards your goal.

In this case my goal is a neat pile of manuscript on which I have just typed 'The End'. These are some of the many tempting actions that will not get me there: Getting up to make a cup of coffee. Taking my ruler and pencil and drawing myself a lovely neat timetable. Sticking little labels on all my files and giving them names. Cutting interesting and possibly relevant articles out of the newspaper. Phoning a friend. No.

All these actions could be useful in the right time and place, but that is not now, not here.

The journey of 1,000 miles begins with a single step, always, without exception. And the step must be in the direction of the goal and not towards the kitchen or the telephone. To have written the book I must begin, in however small a way, to write the book.

I tell the crows to come back again in half an hour, if they must. It is Tuesday morning. I didn't start writing on Monday morning and that's that. Too bad. I have this moment, always this moment. I confront my fears the best way I know how, by naming them. Failure. Ridicule. Inadequacy. Shame. Not being half as clever as I think I am and everybody knowing it. Not being able to sustain what I start. But I have started. The crows have fallen silent. They may be shuffling their feet along the branches, getting ready to croak, but for the moment they have nothing to say. That's what happens when you really begin. Like Indiana Jones stepping out into the chasm, it's only when you really take the first step that the bridge creates itself under your feet.

I must remember, when this happens all over again tomorrow morning, that it's the steps that make the road.

Decoro, Sprezzatura, Grazia

In 1991 I sat in a rehearsal room in Sapporo, Japan, with the dying Leonard Bernstein and had a conversation about the relationship between inspiration and hard work. Bernstein was nearing the end of his life and he was very sick, but I'd just watched him electrifying the London Symphony Orchestra through a rehearsal of Sibelius's First Symphony. Now, with a large Scotch in one hand and a forbidden fatal cigarette in the other, he lay exhausted in the corner of a sofa and talked about the way in which he identified with the composers whose music he conducted. If he'd done his preparation thoroughly, he said, he absorbed the score into his very bones. He could feel that he was composing Beethoven and Mahler anew in the performance. He became the music.

I had an idea to swap with Bernstein, one I'd been given by Anthony Rooley, lutenist and specialist in early music. I told Bernstein that he was talking about the art of *Sprezzatura*, and once I'd explained it to him, he agreed.

The musicians of the seventeenth century, Rooley told me, believed that a great performance had three elements: *Decoro, Sprezzatura and Grazia*.

Decoro is all the preparation and hard work. It's the lonely research, the checking, the rehearsal, repetition and often futile-seeming effort and drudgery which prepare the ground.

Then comes *Sprezzatura*. It is the art of spontaneity. It is the art of standing on the hot spot and performing with such invention and freshness that it is as though the work is flowing through you for the first glorious time. It is the experience of being inspired. This is exactly how Bernstein said he felt about the music he conducted.

Sprezzatura is impossible without *Decoro*. Imagine a mountain. *Decoro* – hard work – is probably nine-tenths of the climb. *Sprezzatura* is the peak – it's magnificent, but you don't hang about there for long. And *Grazia* – divine grace – is the blessed light which illuminates the summit. *Grazia* is what touches a performance in which *Decoro* and *Sprezzatura* are in perfect balance.

But this theory applies to far more than musical performance. It is a Theory of Everything. Leonard Bernstein's life, as I wrote when he died three months later, was a perfect illustration of how these three elements can be the essential ingredients of a successful life as well as a memorable concert. He had astonishing talent but he worked like a dog. His performances, even his rehearsals, were full of *Sprezzatura*, spontaneous to the point of shock. And many people, millions, can testify to the *Grazia*, the grace, that his work teaching, composing and performing brought to their lives.

You don't have to be a kind of genius to use these elements in your life and work. They apply to every kind of human endeavour from sitting school exams to throwing a party to fighting a campaign. *Decoro* without *Sprezzatura* will not do. It is no more than uninspired plodding. But *Sprezzatura* without *Decoro* can lead to the leap which misses the trapeze, the blazing but unprepared talent destroyed by nerves, the dazzling lawyer tripped up by the unexpected question. No *Grazia* there.

Work and play are both essential to human endeavour, but I know from experience that the work comes first. Anyone who has become deeply involved in a project knows that moment when a brilliant creative solution suddenly appears after hours, days or even weeks of labour. Or as Mark Twain said, 'The more I work, the luckier I get.' The luck is *Grazia*. You only get it when you know how to work and then play.

Meditation

People who have no experience of meditation tend to think that it is a matter of sitting and letting your mind go blank. On the contrary. Meditation is the practice of unswerving concentration. It is an intense mental discipline and that is what makes it such a valuable tool in the decluttering of the mind and the destressing of the heart.

Meditation, for those who have embraced it, is as essential to their functioning as *barre* practice to a ballet dancer or scales to a musician. Without it there is no internalized self-discipline to hold everything else together. It was the Dalai Lama who said, 'The more I have to do, the more I meditate.' Meditation means replacing useless fretting and random worrying with a thought-free mental space which allows renewal and change.

The baby meditator has just as much trouble meditating as a baby pianist might have trying to play Beethoven. I am not as regular or as disciplined a meditator as I might be, so this is what often happens when I sit down to meditate. I close my eyes. I focus my attention on the sensation of my breathing. I use a simple sequence of phrases I learned in a retreat led by the Zen Buddhist monk Thich Nhat Hanh. Breathing in, I know that I am breathing in. Breathing out, I know that I am breathing out. Breathing in, I remember that I didn't finish clearing up the kitchen which leads me to the fact that we've run out of bread and before I know it my mind is racing down the high street and into the supermarket. I pull myself up. I focus again on my breath. Breathing in, I am breathing in. Breathing out, I am out tonight because I'm meeting friends for a drink. I must remember to return that book I borrowed and would I be better taking the car, which means finding somewhere to park, and my friend got towed away last time, which means a £200 fine, and … I focus on my breath again.

And so it goes. And so goes everyone. Controlling thoughts is like herding cats. Push them out and they come right back through the cat flap, bringing other stray cats with them. That is why we need to meditate.

When my mind is at its most random and overloaded, victim of the need to multi-task, active in a frantic way like a randomly disfunctioning radio tuner, that is when I need to meditate. When I have a sensation of anxiety deep inside, a feeling that I daren't stop, that is when I need to meditate. When I realize that my thoughts, perhaps about another person or a relationship which is in trouble, are obsessive and repetitive, that is when I need to meditate.

To meditate is to return to a state of still potential out of which organization and order can grow. And it can help order us on the physical level too. I know for a fact, because I check it, that meditation immediately lowers my blood pressure.

Like all regular practices, meditation can create long-term changes in attitude and behaviour. The regular experience of internal stillness and calm creates a recognition and knowledge of the state that can draw you back in times of turmoil. People who are meditators have a tool which can prevent them from acting out their inner turbulence in a way which harms themselves and others. This is why meditation can be so effective when it is taught in prisons and workplaces.

There are many, many ways to meditate. By this I mean ways to attain a state of inner focus and concentration. Musicians, dancers, sportspeople, craftspeople, children lost in a game, anyone whose work requires concentration knows what it is like to get into a meditative state. But the meditative state can be experienced anywhere. The ultimate aim of mindfulness meditation is to make each moment of daily life – preparing breakfast, doing the dishes – an act of mindfulness. By 'mindfulness' I mean nothing more complex, or more difficult, than the simple art of doing and thinking about one thing at a time.

If you have never tried meditation, here is a very simple way to begin.

It is the way I always follow. Find a quiet, undisturbed place to sit. Sit upright. Relax your hands loosely on your knees. Close your eyes. Become aware of your breathing. Simply concentrate on your breath without attempting to control it. Be aware of the sensation of the incoming breath in your nostrils, in your throat, in the rise of your ribs and stomach. When the impulse to release the breath occurs naturally, simply observe the same process in reverse. That is all. Simply observe, without interference, the sensations of your own breathing.

The breath is there to save you from distraction. Hardly will you have started this simple process than your mind will take you anywhere but where you are trying to be, within yourself at this particular moment. It is shocking how hard it is to focus on one simple thing. It is humiliating how easy it is for the unconscious chain reaction of our own random thoughts to take charge of the space of our mind.

But our thoughts are not in charge of our mind. We are. Meditation is the process of discovering, isolating and strengthening this 'we', this 'I', this calm, detached, compassionate observer that need not be swept away in the chaos of our lives. Meditation is the art of building an inner lighthouse to guide us home in the turbulence.

The 'Nice Letters' File

Some time ago, when people wrote more letters than they do now, I began to keep the friendliest and put them in a file. I put a label on the cover and wrote the words 'Nice Letters'. I still have the file, which has grown, and every now and then I add to it – a thank you letter, an affectionate postcard from a friend, a swiftly scribbled pencil note on the back of an envelope written by a departing lodger to tell me how happy he'd been living in my house and how he'd felt like part of my family.

As a journalist with a regular column I attracted more letters than most people and I was always touched when people bothered to be nice. Into my 'Nice Letters' file went congratulatory notes from editors and supportive letters from readers, sometimes sharing a personal experience they thought I would understand. One regular even wrote me funny poems. I still get a kick out of those people who bothered to write down and post the fact that, at a particular moment, I'd done a good job, written something perceptive or memorable, cheered them up, got something right. These letters are a record of all the good things, the little indicators that I was on the right road.

Of course a lot of my letters weren't nice at all. Some readers were horrid, not to say barking mad. I even had a letter from one particularly unhinged reader threatening me with violence and rape. And most of my domestic post is like yours: bills, unsolicited offers of expensive credit, bank statements. Open too many of these in a morning and you can feel your life force ebb away. And that's when you need to open your 'Nice Letters' file and reinforce your self-belief and your belief in the kindness of others.

Nice letters are like a savings bank of testimonials. They're champagne on paper, a reflection of the person as I'd like to be and sometimes am. As for the bad stuff, the heart-sinkers, they go straight in the bin.

What happens to nice letters in a world of e-mails and texts? I know plenty of people who save good e-mails. I suggest you print them out and file them, because there's nothing like hard copy. And don't stop writing letters. No e-mail has the force, the surprise element, the durability of a handwritten letter in a nice envelope falling on the mat.

This isn't about being vain. It's about bottling encouragement and reminding yourself that if you've got it right before, you can get it right again.

Observe your Passion

'It's easy for you,' my friends used to say, 'you have a talent.' What they meant was that they didn't know what to do with their lives. There was no obvious career path, no driving desire, no vision leading them on or ambition energizing them.

Yes, I was lucky. I always knew that I wanted to write, and I had a talent for it too, but having a talent doesn't necessarily mean that you know how to use it. A talent is nothing without passion and I've come to think that when it comes to knowing what you want to do with your life, passion is the best guide of all. Skill can follow.

I started to write this piece because I was thinking of my daughter. I once watched her radiating animation and enthusiasm as she talked about all the things she found exciting that week. When she'd finished, she deflated, sunk her head down and said sorrowfully, 'I don't know what to do with my life.' I told her to listen to herself. She *did* know. Every fibre of her body knew. All she had to do was listen to her passion. So it's a small cosmic joke that she rang me up five minutes ago (and two years after that original conversation), hugely excited, to tell me that a radio station was so impressed with the passion which she and her friends brought to their ideas that they were going to be given their own hour-long slot each week called – of all things – *Passions,* in which they could interview anyone they liked about what made their heart sing. You couldn't make it up.

People who feel at a loss tend to go round asking other people what they should do. I've learned to pay attention to myself. Passion is physical and it's hard information. Is my heart beating faster? Am I talking quickly because my ideas are piling up so fast? Is it difficult to switch off? Do I feel more alive? These are very powerful clues that this is a subject, an area, a project that I could put my heart into. It doesn't matter what other people think you ought to do, or what would be sensible to do, or what fits their idea of you. If you can't get enthusiastic about something, you're not going to put your heart into it. Do the research. Get the education. Do the maths. But if you want the whole picture, listen to your body.

The Magic of 20 Minutes

When people learn that I'm writing a book about everything I've ever done that worked they are puzzled and polite. I try to explain that it's not about how to unblock the sink, more about how to unblock themselves. If you were really stuck in a place you didn't like – a bad relationship, an unfulfilling job, a work crisis, a creative impasse, an emotional loop – and something in this book got you unstuck and flowing, I would call that a result.

When people hear this, they go a bit quiet. Then they might say, 'Have you got anything about being blocked?' Or, 'Have you got anything to help creativity?' Or, 'My biggest problem is focus.' Or, 'I'm so overloaded, I could cry at any minute.' To all of them I would say, 'Yes, I know a trick or two that can help. Try writing a letter to God, try the Emotional Freedom Technique, try expressing gratitude, even when you're feeling overwhelmed by fear. Try writing it down. Above all, try pulling focus. Get very, very small. Get as small as 20 minutes.'

When I feel stuck or unfocused or miserable, everything feels huge and insurmountable. The problem I'm blocked on seems overwhelming and too big to tackle. And what this makes me feel is that I can't, and don't want to do it at all. My resistance is huge so I'll put it off till tomorrow, or some time when I feel like it. That's what 'procrastination' means, by the way. *Pro. Cras*. For Tomorrow.

And we all know when tomorrow comes – never. Which is why the problem doesn't get solved, the focus doesn't get pulled, the great creative breakthrough doesn't happen, ever.

What works is to do the smallest possible thing you can contemplate doing. Can you sit down and write a symphony? No. Can you write a movement? No. Could you write a few bars, 20 minutes' worth? Could you sit at your piano or your music paper for 20 minutes, undistracted by fear, self-criticism, other tasks? It's only 20 minutes. Yes, you could do that. And having done that you might find you could manage five minutes more. And so on.

Never underestimate the power of inertia. It takes far more energy and fuel for a plane to take off than it does to cruise. Cruising is the easy bit. That's why the kind of people who finish projects have many ways to get themselves onto the runway and taxiing off. Some writers finish work in the middle of a sentence so that they can start again the next morning. Some begin by writing their own name over and over until their hand and brain start to write something more interesting.

Above all, you have to stay where you are. Artists go into their studios and stay there, pottering, going through the motions, until something clicks in and ideas begin to work. It might take all day for an original idea to happen, but the action of turning up in the studio or at the desk and staying there lets your unconscious know that you're serious. It's like unblocking a sink, after all. Nothing happens and nothing happens, but you keep trying and then, with a glug and a burp, things start moving. And it's the small things, the increments of 20 minutes, that can bring the shift.

Journalism taught me that the breakthrough often comes with the one extra phone call you don't feel like making. You're getting nowhere and you want to give up and then the last question in the interview gives you the extra insight, the one great quote you've been waiting for. Art training taught me that the creative solution or original idea comes when you're tired and working, not when you are planning a project from the outside. Somehow, if you stick with the work, you reach a point where your controlling mind let's go and a fresh connection sparks. It often happens when I say to myself, 'I'll just do another 20 minutes.'

Whatever it is, you have to be there, with your attention focused. Even, let's say, if you're in the biggest emotional mess and you don't know where to turn or how to think, allow yourself to really feel, really express, sob, howl, rage for 20 minutes and you may find that 20 minutes will take you through to a temporary calm, a small clearing where you can begin to think straight. And after that, another 5, another 20...

It's about leverage. Archimedes said that if he had a place to stand he could move the world. In a tumultuous, frustrating, intransigent world, 20 minutes is our place to stand.

Your Life as a Spiritual Journey

It came in a list of homework to do before a week's workshop: 'Write an account of your life as a spiritual journey.' I was so taken aback that I put it to one side. I couldn't think how to begin.

I wasn't in the habit of thinking of my life in spiritual terms at all. Biographical, yes. Born here. Lived there. Met this person. Had these relationships. Did that job. I could see my life as a constantly updated cv. I could list educational qualifications and professional achievements. I could see my life as doctor's notes: had measles, two pregnancies, broke ankle. I could see my life as a chain of addresses or a series of attachments and relationships. But could I see my life as a spiritual journey? Not without a lot more thought.

Off the top of my head I probably thought that my life was all those things – personal, geographical, professional, emotional – with, now I came to think of it, moments of what could possibly be spiritual experience occasionally slotted in. But I had never thought that these moments might add up to a journey, that there might be any sense of progress or momentum or continuity. I had never thought that so many elements of my daily life would prove to have a spiritual dimension which, I realized, was immensely important to me.

The exercise of sitting down and looking at my life as a spiritual journey was a revelation. It made me look at my whole life in a completely new light. It taught me a great deal about the deeper values which underlay everything I did. It explained to me why there had been periods of my life when I had felt lost and unhappy even though everything had looked good on the surface. Job – fine. Money – fine. Family – fine. Expression of spiritual values – not fine at all.

First, it didn't involve a lot of church-going, though church-going surrounded me when I was a child. I had Welsh grandparents who took me to chapel when I stayed with them and I went to a Church of England primary school where the vicar came in to give a service in the school hall on Wednesday mornings. Yet none of this made me feel holy. Whatever God was, I experienced it, like the poet Wordsworth, out in the fields, in the woods, by the sea. And there were certain pieces of music that, inexplicably, could make me cry.

As I looked at my life as a spiritual journey I could see how devoid of spirit much of it was. In particular I could see why my twenties felt so barren under their busyness – all that partying, all that pushing the career forward, all those experimental relationships, but where was the spirit, the moments of quietness and nourishment? I could see how periods of social and professional success were simultaneously spiritual deserts and swamps. No wonder I had secretly felt lost and bewildered. And I saw with perfect clarity that my spiritual life was nourished and expressed through three main strands – music, art and nature. I also saw that a very dark and depressed period in my life coincided with a complete lack of creative expression. Which came first, the lack of creative expression or the lack of contact with my source?

When we met in the workshop we spent a day taking our individual stories and turning them into visual timelines with the help of collage, paints and photographs. Our teacher, Gloria Karpinski, threw us more questions to help us make sense of our jumbled stories. 'Think of your life as a river,' she said. 'What kind of waters were you born into? Serene or turbulent? Fast-flowing or swampy? What were the turning points, the significant bends? Where was the true self that is always there, no matter what is going on? Are there significant people who crop up on your spiritual journey? A teacher or even a stranger can be more important to your spiritual journey than a parent or a close friend.'

By the end of our workshop we had produced 12 completely individual works of art and we had all learned a lot about what it took to make us happy and fulfilled. We had a much stronger sense of purpose.

What I learned was that those portions of my life where I felt most cut off from nature and blocked from a connection with great music and art were the places where I felt most adrift. I hadn't realized how important music was to me, but there it was, cropping up in my timeline again and again, like a life raft. Somehow these connections affected my whole sense of the meaning of life.

This exercise showed me vividly how it is possible to have all the things the culture says you must have and yet still feel a profound sense of loss and dislocation. What is so striking about it is that you can see exactly where and why this loss and dislocation occurs.

Meaning and happiness, as millennia of saints, artists and philosophers have said, do not lie in wealth, status and possessions. For you they may lie in a mainstream religious practice. For me they don't. Try writing the story of your life as a spiritual journey and, if you didn't know before, you will see where your heart really lies.

'To Do' Lists

I was taught how to make lists by Superwoman. I was a scatty girl in my first job as design assistant to Shirley Conran, a woman who much later became famous as the author of a book which told everyone how to organize their lives. Well, she organized me first.

Shirley's life was ruled by lists. She would pin her demands for the day up on the wall for the rest of us to read and do. 'Give me your six best tips on clutter. I want your six best jokes about weight loss. Give me six ideas on bedrooms.' She also taught us how to keep the lists tidy by crossing each item off with a little vertical line. That way you could instantly see what hadn't been done and when you'd crossed everything on your list off you would get an unbroken vertical line.

Since then I have lived my life by 'to do' lists. At the start of each year, each week, each day or simply when I feel overloaded and in need of a fresh start, I write the date at the top of a page and then write down everything I have to do. I usually have two separate columns, one for work, one for personal tasks. Then, if I'm being really organized, I draw up a timetable for the day or the week, calculate how long each task will take and put it in. Things are more likely to get done if I bother to do this. And the time frame helps enormously. When you see that the phone call you really don't feel like making is only going to take five minutes, there's no excuse for not putting it at the head of your list and getting it over with.

'To do' lists may seem anally retentive and control freaky if you aren't converted to them already, but if you do them religiously they work brilliantly in reducing that internal sense of clutter and panic and in actually getting things done. And they free your mind up for the really interesting things, like planning your summer holiday.

Knowing What You Want and Asking for It

Assertiveness training was the very first kind of self-development work I ever did. It happened this way. I didn't wake up one morning and think, *Aha, I must become more assertive*. I just thought, *I need help*.

I was at a stage in my life where I was at home with two children under three and a patchy freelance career and I somehow felt I had lost the plot. I had no clue what to do about lost plots, but deep down I thought there must be some way of getting perspective on my life or understanding what I was feeling, so I asked my old friend Ann, who also had two children and a career as an artist and was 10 years older and wiser than I was.

Ann didn't know what I needed either, but she did know a psychologist and workshop leader whose work she thought was very good. Her name was Anne Dickson and when I rang her up she was about to start teaching an eight-week course of assertiveness training, and that is how I found myself, for the first time in my life, sitting with a group of strangers being given the behavioural tools to work out what I wanted in life and, crucially, how to get it without being aggressive, whiney, manipulative or self-defeating.

Assertiveness training turned out to be about clarity and honesty, and the day came, much more quickly than I expected, when I put it into practice and it worked.

Anyone who has small children knows how difficult it can be to work at home. I wanted to be my independent working self and I wanted to earn money and I also wanted to be with my children. My husband thought I'd be much happier if I got out of the house and took a full-time job and made the whole thing organized and clear cut, but I wasn't ready for that. I felt I wanted some kind of relationship with an employer that gave me regular work but didn't take all my time. I fixed myself an interview with a former employer, *The Sunday Times*, to see if they had shift work on the news desk.

As I walked the streets between my house and *The Sunday Times'* office my assertively trained brain began to think about the interview, and this is what I thought: *If you're not careful, you are going to get yourself in deep trouble. News is irregular and out of normal hours. You're going to offer your services and you could end up being at the beck and call of a news desk with no fixed limits, which will make it impossible to plan your time or childcare. There's no point going in there and just say-*

ing you'd love to work for them, because you wouldn't. You've got to be clearer than that. And then this new crisp voice came into my head and said, 'What you want is to go and work on the news desk for two days a week. That would be perfect. You'd get enough money and stimulation and experience and you'd get to spend the rest of your time at home.'

Half an hour later I sat in the news editor's office and found myself saying, 'What I'd really like is to come in and work on the news desk two days a week.'

'Fine,' he said, just like that. 'When could you start?'

I was astonished, though I didn't show it. That week I was able to bounce into my assertiveness training class and say, 'Guess what? This stuff really works.'

That was nearly 20 years ago and I've found the techniques of assertiveness training useful ever since. Whether you're negotiating a job, navigating a sticky patch in a relationship or returning shoddy goods to a shop, it's a great tool for being honest with yourself and clear with other people.

Emotional Freedom Technique

This technique is best described as emotional acupressure. I don't understand why it works and you feel really silly doing it, but it does work. It's the quickest, most accessible tool in the box.

Let me give you an example. I woke today at 3.00 a.m. and, in those few seconds between deep sleep and the piecing together of external sounds and sensations that means wakefulness, I felt an anxious feeling in my solar plexus. Then I realized why I had woken up.

There had been an emotional crisis during the day. It hadn't been mine but that of somebody close to me, somebody who had needed comfort and all the calm and stillness I could muster. When I had gone to bed I had deliberately done what I could to put aside the upset of the day. I'd been walking and swimming too, so I was physically tired, and I had fallen asleep quite quickly. But in the cellular cluster of a human tribe, the pain of one affects everyone. It might not have been my immediate problem, but I knew within five wakeful minutes that unless I did something to regain my peace of mind I was going to have an anxious and sleepless night.

What could I do? The first thing I did was take a few drops of the Australian Bush Remedy Dog Rose of the Wild Forces, which claims to protect people from being over-affected by the turbulence of others. Then, though I didn't really feel like stirring myself awake too much, I thought I would try to clear the anxiety by using Emotional Freedom Technique.

Emotional Freedom Technique always works for me. As the man who taught it to me said, 'It's weird, and you feel like an idiot doing it, but it works.' It involves tapping with the tips of your fingers on certain acupressure points in order to release negative energy. While you do it, you say out loud the feeling you want to get rid of. I learned it on a weight-loss programme, but when I looked it up on the internet I found that it has had many applications since it was first developed by an American engineer called Gary Craig. EFT practitioners use it for combating every kind of negative state from fear of flying to giving up smoking. You can go to a practitioner if you have a complex problem (find one through the internet), but you can do the quick version as first aid for yourself.

The brilliance of EFT is its speed and flexibility. It's taught as a two-minute stress technique. You could do it as an emergency remedy in the middle of a stressful day – but preferably locked in the privacy of a lavatory, because you wouldn't want anybody to see you!

This is what you do. You identify the negative feeling you want to shift. In my case I felt worried, so this is what I did. I said out loud, 'Even though I feel worried, I deeply and completely accept myself.' Repeating these words, I started tapping the chopping edge of my right hand with the three middle fingers of my left hand. I did this at least three times, continuing to say my words out loud.

Then, using the index and middle finger of my right hand, I started tapping acupressure points on my face. And I shortened my ritualistic little sentence to its core, to the feeling I want to shift.

'Feeling worried,' I repeated, as I continued to tap, 'feeling worried, feeling worried,' and these are the points I tapped, in order:

1. The inner edge of the right eyebrow, on the bone.
2. Just above the outer end of the right eyebrow, on the bone.
3. Just on the eye socket bone below the centre of the right eye.
4. The centre of the upper lip just below the nose.
5. The centre of the crease between chin and lower lip.
6. The outer edge of the right clavicle or top rib, just inside the shoulder joint.
7. Just inside the right armpit.

8. Then, still repeating my mantra, I moved back to tapping the right hand, first the outer edge of the thumb, just in line with the nail bed.

9. 10, 11. Then the same place on the index, middle and little fingers.

12. Then the karate chop or outer edge of the hand.

13. Then back to the gamut, the point between the joints of the third and little fingers. This is what you do while you are tapping on the gamut point. Without moving your head, you raise your eyes from floor to ceiling and back, from left to right and back, and in a big circle. You hum a few bars of music. You count from one to five. You hum again. Apparently this engages different brain functions. You are then supposed to repeat the round.

Some people suggest you do a kind of audit on yourself by using something called Subjective Units of Disturbance. I find this quite a useful way of assessing a problem anyway. How it works is that you assess your problem on a scale of 0 to 10, 10 being really painful, 0 being bliss. When you've completed your rounds, you reassess. Invariably you feel better. If you don't think you feel better enough, you repeat the process.

This is all very cumbersome to write about, but very easy to do. On this particular night it was all it took to calm myself. Two rounds of tapping. One minute 30 seconds. I could feel my brain disengage from the problem. I put the light out. When I woke up again it was 7.30.

Make Friends with Money

Money and sex are the two issues we find it hardest to talk about, the two issues that break up the most marriages. Which is the bigger taboo? Which is hardly ever taught in schools? Which gives you the bigger jolt of fear on a regular basis? Which are you more likely to lie awake worrying about? Which are you most willing to sweep under the carpet or leave to somebody else to take care of? Which produces the most sense of panic and helplessness? Yes, it's not sex. It's money.

It works to make friends with money. It's going to be your daily concern for the whole of your life, so it doesn't make sense to ignore it or leave it to other people. Even at the start of your working career there are ways to budget, to manage your debts, to organize your savings, to work out how much you need to spend and how much to put aside for the future. Above all, you need to know how to avoid expensive debts.

I'm not going to go into all of this here, because there are plenty of good books about basic financial management. There are excellent money sections in the newspapers aimed at ordinary people with ordinary lives and ordinary incomes. There are agencies, like the Citizens' Advice Bureau, which can help you restructure loan repayments. There are independent financial advisors who are not in the pay of institutions and who are bound to disclose what commission they get on selling you financial products. Beware of advice from institutions, like banks, which have a vested interest in selling you their own products. Their advice is not disinterested. Money is their business and they make it on the loans and products they persuade you to take out.

Taking charge of your money – knowing where it is coming from, where it is going and exactly what you are spending and saving – is hugely important for your sense of independence and self-worth. It doesn't matter who you are, how you see yourself, how unworldly and non-materialistic you want to be, you can't get away with ignoring it. I've observed that those people who think they are above and beyond money are usually very reliant on other people's. Don't be like that. It's just not grown up and it loses you friends.

Getting in a muddle and losing control of your finances can lead to dread, confusion and despair. Never ignore a financial problem, because it will grow in the dark. The sooner you admit to it and communicate with the relevant people, the easier it is to resolve. Non-communication drives financial institutions mad and they will penalize you even more heavily.

If your money is in a muddle, the only way to start gaining control of it is with a day of reckoning. Start by honestly keeping an account of everything you spend, day by day. You'll soon see where the money is going. And go through your bank statements, item by item. You may be one of those people who would rather earn more than spend less, but unless you keep an account of your getting and spending, how will you ever know where to begin?

Your relationship with money is one of the most important in your life and, as with all relationships, truth is the only basis that works.

And, as a rule of thumb, it's always better to make it than take it.

When the Sea is Rough, Mend your Sails

Sometimes nothing seems to be working. You're between jobs. You're in a relationship desert. You're trying to get projects off the ground but nobody is returning your calls. You should be training for a marathon, but you've turned your ankle. You're longing to move home, but deals keep falling through. You've reached the stage where you would even give up and go with the flow if you could, but there is no flow.

Sometimes life is just like that. If, when you look clearly at the situation, you seem to be making the right moves and the world isn't responding, it may be time to take the desperation out of your voice and eyes and respond to the deeper rhythm of events. You may have entered a period of winter. Winter isn't terminal, it isn't death. It's simply time to hibernate, to turn your energy inward and do your growing underground.

Westernized culture doesn't support hibernation. People lead global 24-hour lives where nothing ever sleeps. TV, radio, news, transport, light, heat, internet all keep going like a funfair. Nothing switches off any more and life is full on, or seems to be, so when it goes quiet for us it seems like a violation of the natural order, but it isn't.

Outside the industrialized, computerized world, whether you go back in time or sideways into different cultures, people understand the slower rhythms of life much better than we do. 'To everything there is a season,' says the Bible. Gardeners know it. Fishermen know it. Sailors, farmers, nomads know it. If you look closely at your own life you can see it too. The rhythm changes. Sometimes things flourish, events pile up. Sometimes life feels as though it's gone into slow motion, even stopped.

I've found that the way to survive the little winters of life is to keep working but to reduce your activity and greatly reduce your expectations. At times like these it never works to force anything. When the sea is rough, mend your sails. When the ground is frozen, live off your harvest. When you can't take the herds into the pasture, give them hay and stay by the fire and weave your rugs or mend your tents.

Assuming you're not a fisherman or a nomad, there are plenty of things you can do in times of hibernation. These are times for editing your possessions, harvesting your resources, evaluating your progress, learning new skills, cultivating friendships, catching up on reading or sleep, caring for your body, going within and reconnecting with your dreams. There may be lessons to be learned and now you have the time to learn them. Your maps may need to be redrawn and now you have the time to redraw them, knowing all the time that the season and the energy will shift.

As spring follows winter, times of inactivity are followed by times where your feet don't touch the ground. A season in the wilderness, which can happen to the most gifted, famous and celebrated people, can quickly become a call back to the market-place. And when the call comes, you'll be prepared, because one thing you do in times of inactivity is keep faith with yourself, your abilities and your dreams. You keep preparing, so that when the change comes, as it always does, you are ready to respond. And the next time the signs of winter come round you can recognize and greet them without fear.

Be a Music Listener

I was standing on a crowded platform waiting for a train into work and I was reading a magazine that had come through the morning post. In it there was an article which quoted the American composer John Cage and it changed my openness to life in an instant. Somebody had asked Cage what his definition of music was. 'Music,' he said, 'is whatever I hear when I put myself in the frame of mind to be a music listener.'

I looked up from my magazine, suddenly enchanted. If music was what you heard when you put yourself in the frame of mind to be a music listener, then this grimly crowded suburban Tube station in the rush hour must be a source of music.

I put myself in the frame of mind to be a music listener. I picked up the rhythm of an incoming train, a bass line. I layered in the brassy squealing of its brakes. A vocal line came from the amplified announcement overheard. There was the choral counterpoint of a dozen different conversations, the soft percussion of feet shuffling on the platform, the woodwind of blackbirds in the sycamore trees by the track, the cooing and ruffling of pigeons in the roofbeams.

Suddenly, by this simple shift in perception, the day was transformed. The mundane, unpoetic world of the station was full of magic. Better, this magic, this limitless source of everyday music, was available to me anywhere, any time. No matter where I was, I simply had to put myself in the frame of mind to be a music listener.

Later that summer I took a holiday on Crete. The village I stayed in could only be reached by boat or precipitous mountain path. Its soundscape was the same as that which would have been heard by the Minoans thousands of years earlier. I heard the gentle folding of the tideless crystal-clear water on the stones of the beach. I heard the cooing of wood pigeons in the olive trees. I heard the stereophonic clonking of goat bells from the goats scattered over the steep mountainside, and twice a day the single chimes and clanks turned into a great tintinnabulation as the single goats gathered into a rushing headlong flock pouring down the mountain to be fed by the water's edge.

There were moments on that holiday when I deliberately sat down in the shade of an olive tree to be a music listener and found that the waves and the goat bells and the birds weren't the half of it. The notes I took under my olive tree bring the experience back more clearly than any photograph:

The music of Loutro. Jazz guitar, *pianissimo*, from the bar next
door. Clank, clang, goat bells from the cliff across the water. Goat
bleat, across the water, faint. Splash, swoosh, slip slap, the sea on
the quayside. Boat engine, a new note, *diminuendo*, cuts out.
Chopping, hammering from a restaurant kitchen. Slurp, squelch,
the sea. Whistling, chirruping, trilling, canary in a cage. Metallic
hammering. Distant bleat. Very faint goat bell. Clink, fork on plate.
Rattle, clatter, clunk, a man walks by carrying a crate of bottles along
the quay. Soft clunk, a fridge door closes. Dog barks. Woodwind
of small birdsong in the tamarisks, blackbirds and sparrows. The
underlying hum of refrigerators full of cold drinks and fresh fish.
The fridge note rises and the thermostat kicks in.

When you listen this intently, wonderful things happen. Your ear
becomes attuned to subtle sounds, the constant unnoticed accompaniment of
your day. Your mind becomes suddenly aware of something even more subtle. I
began to understand that the world must be full of sounds we can't hear. All
around us extraordinary things are happening which radiate a silent energy.
They must have a sound, but our ears are not designed to hear it. I've read since
that sound recordists working in north Yorkshire recorded 54 separate sounds of

water in the waterfalls and rivers on the moors. I've heard a vulcanologist talk about the deep song a volcano sings as it builds up to an eruption.

As the days went past in Crete and I played this game more deeply I began to keep a parallel page of notes I headed 'Silent Movie'. The Silent Movie of the quayside in the evening went like this:

> I can't hear the sound of the sun setting, the sound of the colour changing on the hills, the sound of the seaweed growing under the clear water, the sound of the little grey fish changing direction.

> I can't hear the mountains shifting, the peaks growing smaller, the moon rising (though it must make a tremendous roar). I can't hear the darkness falling, the night thickening, the shadow creeping across the mountain. I can't hear the sound of the gold wine trembling in the glass. I can't hear the sound of the sea becoming lighter than the sky or the sound of the day's heat escaping from the stone.

Of course a Greek island is full of magic, but you can be a music listener anywhere where – and this is a huge irony – music is not playing. The surest way to dull your ears and kill this particular source of music, to break this subtle connection between yourself and the song of the turning world, is to drown it out with amplified sound. If any of those Greek *tavernas* had been playing loud music I would have lost the experience of one of the most magical sounds anywhere: the beehive hum of human voices rising in one collective village-sized conversation.

Everyone should try putting themselves in the frame of mind to be a music listener. It is one way to discover that a seemingly barren landscape is full of life, that the seemingly inert is endlessly dynamic, that the mundane is miraculous.

Let Others Say 'No'

Have you ever seen a two year old have a tantrum? It's an awesome sight, a small human tornado of rage, protest and affronted dignity. Two year olds don't have tantrums because they're bad people. They have tantrums because they are being confronted with the power of No and everything in them is screaming 'No' right back.

But that external No wins in the end and it wins by getting right inside the two year old and setting up home for life. Growing up is a long process of learning what and what not to do and most of us get it in the end, though you do sometimes see adults throw a tantrum because they're not getting their own way. It's a horrid sight and, thank goodness, very rare. Most of us have been socialized well enough to control our own morality and behaviour. We know how to keep the lid on ourselves. This is good and wise behaviour for a two year old, but as we grow older it has its drawbacks. There are situations where self-censorship not only does us no good, it positively holds us back. We become too self-controlled for our own good.

I'm talking about ambition, creativity, adventure, self-expression, originality, breaking the rules. If we've been too thoroughly squashed we'll have a whole chorus of inner voices going, 'That's no good,' 'Who do you think you are?' 'You can't do that, what will people think?' and 'People don't do that. Nobody's done that before.' Those inner voices stop us doing bad things, but they can stop us doing good things too. The fact is that nothing worthwhile or interesting gets done in this world until people learn to deafen themselves to some of those controlling voices.

It's the fact that these voices are *inside us* that does all the damage. I have found that life frees up a lot when you get them out of your head and leave the criticism to the 'everyone' that's supposed to be delivering it in the first place.

I've got a mantra for this. It's 'Let other people say "No".' Ignore all the No-sayers inside you and put your ideas and desires out there. What's the worst that can happen? You'll get rejected? People will think you're an idiot? Is that worse than living with a constant chorus of inner rejection? Is it worse than never knowing if your ideas would have worked? Is it worse than not knowing if that girl would have gone out with you or if that new friend would have come to dinner? Let other people say 'No', because the best that can happen is that they'll say 'Yes'.

What's the opposite of a tantrum? I don't really know, but it could be the explosion of surprise and delight when you break the depressing habit of saying 'No' to yourself and find that the world is saying 'Yes' to you after all.

The Beauty of Boredom

Boredom must be worse than pain, because I see people heading willingly towards hurt but most people would do anything to avoid boredom. People will eat too much, take drugs, get drunk, create trouble, hurt each other, commit crimes, anything, anything, no matter how self-destructive or anti-social, to alleviate the horrors of boredom.

What's so bad about being bored? I was really bored just the other day and it was painful. I'd agreed to go to a seminar on contemporary art and one of the speakers, an academic who was presumably being paid for her work, gave the worst lecture I have ever heard. It was stumbling, woolly, incoherent. She'd lost her notes and she'd lost her audience too within five minutes.

It is interesting observing a room full of bored people. Nobody can keep still. Everyone becomes restless and wriggly. They pull their hair and scratch their heads, even hold their head up in their hands to stop it falling off their necks in sheer despair. People began to leave. I couldn't, so I wriggled and doodled and scratched and held my head on with the rest, inwardly screaming for the lecture to end. My life slowed to a near stop. Time almost stood still.

And I thought about all the other things I would rather be doing. I realized, with perfect clarity, what tasks and occupations I would rather be getting on with. So I want to sing the praises of boredom.

Boredom makes your life last longer. Boredom makes you realize what your priorities are. Boredom makes you know, absolutely, as you didn't before, exactly what you would rather be doing. And boredom makes you develop your own inner resources. It is boredom, not necessity, that is often the mother of invention. I can remember Sundays as a child when I could have turned inside out with boredom; afternoons when I'd read my book, done a puzzle and didn't know what else to do with myself. There was no television, no computers, no computer games. In those prehistoric circumstances you had to do what people have always done: become creative.

Next time you're bored, don't run to go shopping or turn on the television. Just sit with it. At the moment when it becomes intolerable you might find yourself doing something new.

Write a Letter to God

I got this idea from Spiritual Fitness coach Caroline Reynolds, who uses it in her workshops. If you don't like the idea of writing a letter to God, and even less the idea of getting a letter back, think of this as yet another way of tapping into your unconscious mind. Caroline says it works just as well if you write it to your Higher Self.

The technique is very simple. Get a pad of paper. Sit down and write a letter beginning 'Dear God'. Then write, without thinking about it too much, whatever situation or problem you'd like help with. Sign it 'Yours gratefully, [your own name]'.

Now, without stopping to think, write your reply straight back:

Dear [Name],

This is how I see your situation.
This is what I think you should do.
Yours ever,
God

Do not stop to rationalize, consider or criticize. Just keep your hand moving. You'll know when to stop. The answer comes from a wiser, more far-seeing, more compassionate voice, speaking above the stress and panic of daily life. It will surprise you. What it says is personal to you and can be a valuable, ever-present source of advice and encouragement.

As an experiment, because I haven't used this technique for a while, I just stopped to write a letter to God about a difficult family situation. I was immediately struck by the way in which the need to explain the situation and my own feelings about it to a God-like adviser made me think it through much more clearly and fairly than before. After all, if God doesn't know when you're fudging the issue or being self-justifying, who does? So writing a letter to God in itself encourages the highest level of clarity, understanding and honesty. As I wrote my letter out, fresh solutions were already coming into my mind, but I ploughed on, ignoring them.

When God wrote back, in my own hand (or when I tapped my own deeper understanding and intuition), it was in a spirit of compassion and wisdom. All at once I could see the other person's point of view and how the situation had arisen. I could see what was unchangeable about the problem and how I could behave to avoid getting hurt by it. I even had some fresh and playful ideas about how to introduce a new note, how to get out of the habitual emotional gridlock. God's answer, written uncritically and without pausing to think, gave me fresh perspective, new thinking, renewed compassion, a sense of hope. And a reminder that there's a valuable technique here that I should use more often.

The advantage of writing a letter to God is that you are taking on the voice of an infinitely wise, all-seeing, all-knowing being with the perspective of eternity. There's a spark of that in all of us and that spark will illuminate your reply.

It's Never Too Late

I met my friend Juliette on a part-time adult education art course. She was a very beautiful girl, a young housewife at home with young children. Eight years later we were sitting round the dinner table of one of our fellow students, having a reunion. In the eight years since we'd first met, Juliette had done a degree in theatrical and film make-up and she had run a team of make-up artists on a major television drama series. Now she was about to apply for a place on an MA Fine Arts degree course at a major London art college. She was about to hit 40, but her face was just as luminous and energized as it had been eight years before. 'It's never too late,' she sang triumphantly. 'I'd just like everyone to know it's never too late.'

It's never too late, not until you're dead. I've just been celebrating my friend David's sixtieth birthday at a party where he told us all he'd finally met and was sharing his life with the love of his life. My former aunt-in-law remarried at the age of 75. My mother started a new career as a teacher at 50. Maybe it's too late if you're an insect. My favourite cartoon shows two mayflies. One is saying to the other, 'It's half past three. We've left it too late to have children.' But we're not mayflies.

Just this morning I tore out the obituary of an artist called William Steig, who became a successful children's author in his sixties and created the monster character Shrek in his eighties. On my pinboard there's a cutting about a happy couple who met and fell in love in their eighties and another about a painter called Edwina Leapman, who composed and recorded her first CD at the age of 70. I once met a millionaire philanthropist and businessman called Ernest Hall who clasped my hand and told me, 'I'm 65 and last year I recorded a CD of piano music by Lutoslawski and Bartok with the Leeds Sinfonia, and I'm only telling you this because if I can do it, anyone can do anything.'

I began to learn that it was never too late when I was in my twenties. Somehow you expect to leave college with all your learning done forever, but life isn't like that, thank goodness. I learned to ride a horse for the first time as an adult because I wanted to go on a horse-riding holiday in Spain. I learned to sight-read music in my forties because I wanted to join a big choir. I went to art school and learned animation in my fifties because I wanted to prove to myself that I could. Who knows what I'm going to learn next?

The only things that make it too late are biological and medical. Zelda Fitzgerald left it too late to be a ballerina in her forties because you just don't get ballerinas that old, though there are many kinds of dance that are more generous to older people. A flamenco dancer once told me that you couldn't be good at flamenco until you were in your fifties because you wouldn't have lived enough. Zelda just chose the wrong dance discipline, because it's never too late to dance.

Just don't be so relaxed that you leave your dearest ambition to the last minute. Health does make a difference. My old English teacher once gave me a single piece of advice, which was never to put things off, because she'd always planned to travel when she retired, but her arthritis became so bad that she couldn't.

Arthritis and travel apart, it's possible to have a new lease of life at any age, and I can't think of anything more cheering, encouraging and optimistic than that.

Embrace the Dragon

My habitual approach to nature is to choose a nice bit and lie down in it. There's nothing I like better than to lie flat on my back in a summer field of long grasses and gaze upwards, thinking, *Hello, Clouds. Hello, Sky*. People who talk about 'pitting themselves against nature' or 'conquering' it seem to have got it all wrong. Can't they see that nature doesn't give a damn? It's themselves they are conquering.

Nevertheless I once spent a week in North Wales abseiling down rock faces and scrambling up icy rivers because I loved someone who loved these things and I thought if I could learn to love them too, we could do them together. What I learned was how to deal with fear (and, later, that if you come at the same experience from the opposite angle as your loved one, you are going to have trouble sharing it).

So my plan didn't work as far as the relationship went, but it did teach me about moving through fear and I did have a fantastic time because I was with a group of people who were as interested in discussing the emotions involved as they were in pot-holing and rock-climbing. (The emotions involved in standing at the top of a high waterfall and being asked to jump? Intense.)

The catchword for the week, the rallying cry, was 'Embrace the dragon', and the dragon was your own personal fear. You notice that they, and I, don't use the word *conquer*. Embracing the dragon rather than conquering it means that the fear continues to exist and you face and include it rather than suppress it. I learned that it is possible to embrace the dragon of fear, act with it and still be afraid. I learned that by abseiling deep down a dark slate mine and only losing my nerve once I was spinning freely on the abseil rope, 50 feet above the ground. I had no choice then but to feed myself down, gibbering, and then climb the steel rope ladder back up again, sobbing. I survived, but there was no sense of triumph.

It was different with the waterfall. There I stood, quivering, at the top, with encouraging helpers up to their necks in icy water in the river below shouting, 'Come on, Lesley, embrace the dragon!' So in the end I jumped. I disappeared beneath the icy water. I surfaced. I was wet, cold, intoxicated, exhilarated. Ever since that day I am that person you see going straight into a cold sea without flinching, annoying her friends by shouting, 'Come on in, it's lovely!' I now know that if they would embrace the dragon of a ten-second pain threshold they would become addicted to the cold-water high that I enjoy.

But when I jumped into that waterfall I learned more than the fact that cold water is only cold water. I learned that most fears are simply imaginings that fence you in. Leap the fence. Open the tax demand. Investigate the noise in the night. Sit and contemplate the spider instead of screaming and closing your eyes. Look at the snake in the zoo with the same open-minded wonder you can bring to a flower.

And if that fails, I still know that you can act through and with fear. I remember hanging on the abseil rope in the dark and clambering up the rope ladder and I know that I can get through a difficult experience if I breathe slowly and consciously and take it one small step at a time.

Look, Look Again

I'm looking at the head of a white anemone in a blue and white vase on the table in front of me. Something makes me stop taking it for granted, put my pen down and really give the flower my full attention. It's a white anemone. That's what my mind says. My mind is like a secretary following me round, taking crisp notes. It's like a clever schoolchild. It loves to label and identify things. Its hand is always up in the air, quivering with easy knowledge. But is it telling me the whole truth? Let me really look.

The flower head is bowing slightly before me, gazing down on the tablecloth. Its petals radiate round a thick tasselled crown of *grey* stamen. Grey, says my mind, shooting up its know-all hand. Let me really look. Those little seedheads, clustered on white filaments, aren't really grey at all. Brown? Mouse? Pale coffee? Actually, I look again and each one is different. At the top, where they are angled towards the light, I can see that each one is white, off-white, cream, round a tiny stripe of green, while at the bottom, they are a dingy cardboard colour, buff, string, the colour of a tax demand envelope.

And is the flower really white? When I look I can see that no petal, no stripe of a petal, is the same colour. The tissue, the flesh of each petal is very fine, so that there is a transparency that takes on the colour of whatever is near it.

There, at the heart, is a faint green blush shining through from the leaf behind. The petal's tip gleams where the light passes through the ultra-fine webbing of veins that gives the petal its structure. The flower is an object of breathtaking fragility, its delicate surfaces crumpled into a complex layering of subtle lights and shades. And it is a radiant force of energy, its paper-thin petals shooting out from its densely seeded heart with a driving force. Whatever that force is, it holds each fine fragile petal in place.

When I pay this much attention to a flower, or to anything else mundane in my view – the subtle gleams of light on a green-glazed dish, the fine weave and shading of a tablecloth, the geography of my own hand – many things happen that are good and helpful.

My habitual thinking mind stops. That is the mind which is continually preoccupied with memory and fantasy, the memory of wrongs done and hurts received, the fantasy of events turning out well or badly.

I am fed with beauty. And I am reminded that beauty isn't something you find in museums or shops. Beauty is all around me, even at my kitchen table.

I'm in awe. In awe is a great place to be. It changes perspective, alters the brain's chemistry, triggers gratitude, creates the space for fresh thinking.

There isn't a moment in the day when this kind of revelation isn't freely available. It's something I learned in art class, where I was taught to look. I was taught, especially, to look at the relationship of one thing to another, at the spaces between things. I was taught to observe the relationship of one colour to another and I learned that what the mind calls blue is 100 other things when you really look. I was taught to *see*.

All the act of seeing takes is the conscious decision to take our attention away from our own internal monologue and our received knowledge and to fix it on something outside in the world, without labelling and preconceptions, if we can.

The reward of attention is revelation.

Gifts of Love

Sometimes you can take something and turn it on its head and something wonderful comes out of it. Creative people – artists, designers, composers – know that if you're truly stuck, changing the scale and perspective and angle of a problem can lead to a whole new source of fresh thinking, an undreamed-of solution. I did this once in my journalistic life and it worked.

I was the women's editor of the *Mail on Sunday* and it was coming up to Christmas. There are no surprises about Christmas pages. They are traditionally crammed with suggestions for presents for him, her, them, the family dog. They are crammed with stocking-filler ideas for over-indulged teenies, luxurious treats for grown ups, expensive objects for people who probably gave the last present you bought them to Oxfam – yes, I know, you can hear the spirit of Scrooge in my voice. There's something about Christmas as a gigantic shopping opportunity that really gets me down.

So I sat in my little glass cubbyhole of an office and I brooded, growing more Scroogelike by the hour. I could feel my annual resistance to the great stuff-and-spend fest growing every minute. *Why do we have all these pages urging people to spend money on things they don't want? I grumped to myself. And then, slowly, Why can't we use these pages to get people to give money instead?*

Why couldn't we use the Christmas pages to get people to give money? Wait a minute. How would we do that? Suppose we asked all those people whose merchandise we would normally be featuring to donate it as prizes. And then we'd pile it all into a photographic studio with kids and dogs and a Christmas tree – as we might anyway. Only this year it would be different. This year everything in the picture – and a lot more that we couldn't get in – would be prizes. To enter, our readers had to ring in and pledge money and the money would all go to the National Society for the Prevention of Cruelty to Children.

I learned a big lesson in the infectious, runaway power of a good idea. Nobody had to be persuaded. The editor loved it. Our advertisers loved it. All the PRs who pledged us prizes loved it. And gradually, everyone in the office loved it. It began in a corner of our office with the fashion department, who were always brilliant at bringing in the stuff everyone wanted, the fashion and beauty treats, but soon people I'd never seen before were sticking their heads round my door saying they knew manufacturers who'd agreed to donate a car or a travel company that would offer a holiday in Fiji.

The photoshoot was hell. Neither the dog nor the children behaved, but the fund-raising was a wild success. The paper put the campaign all over the front page in the week before Christmas. Staff from all over the paper answered the phones and we raised over a quarter of a million pounds, which 20 years ago was worth a huge lot more than it is today. It was the first newspaper Christmas charity campaign and the best result was that now nearly all newspapers run them, though without the prizes. But then they don't have the nice job of ringing up readers and telling them that they've won a holiday in Fiji.

What I want to say is that it is possible to stand resistance and grumpiness on their heads and turn them into something really good. Without my grumpiness about Christmas and a yearning to do something different, a whole purpose-built NSPCC family centre would not have existed. The question that made the difference was not the one I was first asking – 'How can I get out of doing this?' – but the one I asked myself next: 'If this has got to be done anyway, how can I do it differently and make something good out of it?' It's a question I often ask myself when I'm offered work I don't particularly want to do. I may only have used it to raise money once, but it always has transformative power. And if it can't be answered, then I think twice about doing the work.

Find your Own Rhythm

There are many places in the world which still wake, work and sleep to the rhythms of the Earth and sun and seasons. If you travel through Africa or India, beginning your journey before dawn, you see people and their animals stirring awake as the light of the approaching sun catches the first smoke from the cooking fires.

We are designed to do the same – to wake, work and sleep to the universal rhythms around us, being more wakeful and active in summer, hibernating in winter, sleeping in the heat of the day and rising with the sun. The trouble is, the rhythms of the world that most of us know have gone crazy and detached themselves completely from the moon and the stars, and so have we.

What I'm trying to say is that everything changed for us with the Industrial Revolution, when we began to serve the needs of mechanization. The rhythms that drive us have carried on changing with relentless speed ever since. The electric light bulb transformed our ability to work after sundown, in winter darkness. Air travel hurtled us so efficiently and matter-of-factly to distant places that our world is now largely run by jet-lagged people toughing out the disruptive effects of shuttle diplomacy. Computers, telephones and e-mails rudely break time and travel zones and place us all on permanent alert. People used to complain about the nine to five, but for many people, nine to five would be a blessed release. And underneath all this frantic activity we are the same old cavemen, longing to obey the sun.

I carried out an experiment on myself once which has affected the way I've worked ever since. I decided to break out of the nine-to-five orthodoxy and follow the natural rhythms of my own mind and body. I was able to do this because I had taken time off from writing for newspapers in order to write a book. The driving, relentless rhythm of newspapers was difficult to shake off, but I decided, as an experiment, for the space of one week, to wake when I woke, begin work when I felt ready and stop when I felt tired. For that week I was on my own in a rented house with nobody else to look after or impose their own rhythms on me.

Within 48 hours it became perfectly clear how my mind and body liked to operate. I am not a very early riser, however much I wish I were, but the school run had been getting me of bed every day. On my own, I woke around eight, breakfasted and was sitting at my desk at nine. I then worked in a state of perfect concentration until I noticed that outside thoughts were beginning to penetrate. This was normally around two o'clock.

Then I stopped. I had a late lunch. I went out for a walk or to shop. My great discovery was that I seemed to need to take as many hours off as the hours I had already worked. An hour's break wasn't enough, but after four or five hours, in the early evening, I felt ready for another session at my desk. It was a very productive week and a very happy one.

Ever since then I've known that I get most of my work done in the morning. Of course, as soon as I was back home other people's schedules impinged. Newspapers put me back on their deadlines. Children needed ferrying and feeding. Evening social activities used up the energy I had been able to save for work. But I'd got very useful information and now I know this: conventional working hours are a nonsense. Offices pay to have people's bodies sitting there, but their useful, creative, energetic minds are often somewhere else. Ask any freelance. They know they get far more done at home.

The Art of Pulling Focus

Imagine your life is a landscape and you are a bird. Down on the ground or in a treetop you have no sense of the whole. All you can see are grass stalks or twigs and leaves and the food that lives there.

Take off up into the sky and everything is clear. You see the grass in relation to the trees, you see the trees in relation to the ground. You see this valley and the curve that leads to the one beyond. You see the glint of water and the shape of the hunting cat.

Fly higher and you see the curve of the horizon and the nature of the approaching weather. You begin to get a sense of worlds beyond the valley and you can catch the signals that tell you to head south to your invisible but persistently calling destination. But you can't live up there. When you need to eat you must go down near the ground again and deal with the urgency of survival, and you risk losing your sense of the whole, your perspective and your sense of destination.

I've learned that the art of successful living calls on the ability to pull focus on these three levels of reality: the calling of the long-distance goal and the sense of something much bigger than my own life, the overview of the elements of my own life and the essential art of operating among the grass stalks of detailed reality.

Some people can operate brilliantly at all levels because somehow, in the chaos, they can still refer to the bird's eye view in their head and heart and see how everything relates. I can't do that. I need to pull back from time to time, away from the overwhelming detail and the overload of calls for my attention, and refocus.

I'm not alone in this. Spiritual disciplines have always advocated retreats to reconnect with God or non-material values. It's common now for big companies and organizations to pick out those staff who need the overview and send them off on retreats and seminars to refocus and recharge. People who work alone need to remember this too. So you can't afford a week's retreat or a workshop or the services of a coach. You can afford to take a day out, a kind of vision quest where you carry one question in your mind – *What do I do next?* – and let it simmer there while you go hillwalking or meditate or look at art. Even an hour where you shut the world out can make a difference.

When people who have pulled back to regain their sense of direction begin to refocus in close-up mode they need to connect their sense of wider vision with the demands of the everyday world. They need to have a strategy which connects the bird's eye view with the demanding short-term world of the grass stalks. I find it helps to have to answer the question *What can I do in the next 20 minutes that will take me in the direction I want to go*? It could be writing a letter, making a phone call, paying off a debt, filling a bin liner with rubbish, joining Weight Watchers, starting a file for a project, delegating a project to somebody else. But it mustn't be big. It should be writing an A4 outline of a novel, not 'I'm going to write a novel'. Thinking too big on the ground only leads to paralysis.

These are the guidelines. Think very big. Think very small. Learn to go back and forth easily between different lengths of focus. Think horizons and weather systems. Think grass stalks and twigs. If you stay in the clouds, you won't eat. If you stay on the ground, you might get eaten. If you dream too much, you'll get lost in inertia because nothing you try will measure up to your dream. If you are run off your feet with the detail and other people's demands, you're in danger of losing your inner map, your bigger picture, the one only you can possibly know about until you begin to make it public. If and when you do, you might become one of those rare people, the ones whose bigger dreams drive and inspire others.

The Seduction of Overload

I look back through my diaries to a time when I lived in a permanent state of overload. I was a single parent. I seemed to be writing a ludicrous number of articles. Unless I was lying to my own diary, I was sometimes dashing off two and three a day. I was singing in a big choir and hurtling off to rehearsals and concerts. My emotional life was a mess. I was constantly telling myself and anybody who asked how exhausted I was and I was longing to sink into some kind of oblivion. I was desperate for time to myself and yet I seemed to feel I wasn't spending enough time with my children. I constantly felt it was my job to keep everyone around me happy. What did I think I was doing?

I was in the grip of an addiction, the addiction of overload. And once an overload addict, always an overload addict, just like being an alcoholic.

The thing about overload addiction is that it feels so right. A person who is overloaded will complain about being tired and having no time, but be triumphant in their inability to offload. The payoffs for their state are huge. Life feels so exciting and full. The overloaded person feels alive. They are needed, wanted, in demand. Overload clicks right into the rigours of the Protestant work ethic. Thou shalt not slack. So, as the overloaded person staggers from appointment to appointment, they take pride in their stress. It is a badge of honour to have a full diary, to juggle work and children, to be exhausted. The overloaded person's place in the world is fully justified. They may feel the guilt of letting friends and family down, but they don't feel the guilt of being unproductive. Who needs any of the other narcotics life offers when you are running on pure, self-generated adrenalin?

Addiction to adrenalin is like any other addiction. Its highs are followed by downs. My diaries tell me that my frantic cramming in of work, activity and experience was punctuated with times when I felt as though I had been hit with a sledge hammer. The weeks when I filed copy like a medium on speed were followed by days when the work I was doing was effortful and sub-standard. The intoxication and exhilaration of my emotional roller-coaster were followed by days of tearful depression.

A life of adrenalin and overload is thrilling, even fulfilling, but it is not sustainable. Sooner or later something snaps: dates are broken, deadlines overshot, friendships and family relationships compromised and neglected. Worst of all, your mind and body are damaged.

The first step to overload recovery is recognition. Nothing happens without that moment of personal clarity when the overloaded person says, 'I can't go on like this.' This is usually accompanied by feelings of despair and frustration because it is impossible to see how the pattern can be broken. At that point you are on the roller-coaster and it is very hard to get off, though illness gets you off it, always. The mind may be driven, but the body will only put up with so much.

Sometimes people know this and ignore it. I was in the office of a very successful magazine editor who hadn't taken a holiday in 10 years. She had come to hate her job. 'The only way I'll get out of here is on a stretcher,' she said. I tried to persuade her that it might be better to take a holiday. Luckily, she decided to quit before the breakdown happened, but it was only just in time. Do you really want to be rescued by a heart attack or a car crash?

If overload is your problem, apply the 20-minute rule. You can't stop the roller-coaster right now this minute, but you can walk round the block. Ask yourself, 'Is this really what I want to be doing?' If the answer is 'Yes', ask yourself, 'Am I willing to pay the price for doing it this way?' There is always a price, usually in health, often in compromised relationships. Ask yourself another question: 'Am I willing for those close to me to pay the price?' This is harder to answer, especially if your overload is providing material benefits for your family. It is quite possible that you haven't clocked that others are paying a price (though they may have been trying to tell you). Your answer might still be 'Yes.'

Anyway, even if the answer is 'No' or 'Maybe not, but what can I do?', you can see no way out. You are indispensable. Other people depend on you. Your cause will fail, your project collapse without you. Know that these delusions are also symptoms of overload. If sickness struck, you would find that people would manage, even blossom, without you.

If you have answered 'No' to any of these questions, know that you need more time and that you must begin to find some somehow. When recognition of overload struck me, I found a therapist and carved two hours out of the week to see her. Change arises out of the still points.

A huge component of change is the art of saying 'No'. You can start saying 'No' to the future right away, but in the meantime you must still deal with all the things you've said 'Yes' to. Before the art of saying 'No' comes the art of graceful disentanglement. Know that if you don't do this voluntarily you may end up doing it anyway, like the hardworking friend of mine who suddenly discovered she had cancer. Now she has cleared her diary for a whole year to nurture herself in a way she didn't take time for before. Now is the time to learn to delegate.

Do you really have to do all this stuff single-handed?

A calmer, less adrenalin-fuelled life can be built with small increments of time. Take the moment to notice what your life is really like. Take five minutes to book an appointment with a doctor, therapist or life coach or arrange a walk with a friend. Take 20 minutes to leave the computer and walk round the block. An hour to read and think. An hour for the gym or a yoga class. A weekend away. A holiday.

Relinquishing dependence on adrenalin isn't easy, but remember that adrenalin is the chemical of danger. It's safe and exciting to experience its intoxication through controlled circumstances like sport or dance. It is not safe to let it run your life.

West Cork Time

West Cork does it for me. It's a magical corner of south-west Ireland where landscape is weatherscape. It's both timeless and in constant motion. Clouds drift perpetually overhead from the vast spaces of the Atlantic. The tide constantly flows and ebbs on almost empty beaches, leaving its rippling signature on the sand. You can sit on clifftops, rocky promontories, in ancient stone circles, and feel suspended in time, en-tranced. Landscape and skyscape are the narcotics that soothe all your worries away.

I once spent two weeks in West Cork, endlessly paddling in clear water and lying on my back looking at the sailing clouds until I felt the world reverse and that I was hovering in a green sky looking down on the blue. When I returned to the city I felt wonderfully calm and optimistic until the city began to rush in at me in all its panic and urgency.

But this time I had a mantra. 'West Cork Time,' I'd say to myself and the urgency would creep back like an ebbing tide. Instantly my eyes would look skywards from a crowded pavement and find the clouds that float over cities too. My heart rate would slow and my blood pressure fall. Inside myself I tuned into timelessness, and the pressure of the city sighed and deflated.

Of course, if you live in a city, its insistent rhythms and human conflicts will demand that you respond to them on their terms sooner or later. But West Cork Time never goes away. It's always there as a resource. Maybe for you it's Caribbean Time or Kerala Time or Aegean Time. You know what I mean. It's time that's too big to be measured on clocks and it never runs out.

Lead a Double Life

I was in my early twenties when I first cottoned on to the fact that people can think you're somewhere when you're not. This was a really useful discovery that I've gone on refining and applying ever since. You too can be your own alter ego. You too can lead a double life.

I first learned the lesson because I'm not great at late nights. One day I overcame the fear of upsetting my friends and being a boring party pooper and I simply slipped away from a party earlier than everyone else. And that's when I realized that nobody really notices. The secret is to register a presence and then rely on the fact that most people are far too busy having their own experience to notice that you're not there having it with them.

I then found that this virtual presence continued to operate even if I went away for a whole year. Even if I went off to another country altogether. I went off to travel round Africa and to live in Ethiopia. The received wisdom is that you mustn't go away or abandon your career or fall out of the loop. The wisdom I learned is that, again, nobody much notices. When I came back from Africa it was as though I'd popped round the corner for a loaf of bread. Everyone in my world had been so busy getting on with their own lives that, apart from really close friends and family of course, they hadn't really registered my absence.

The same thing happened to a friend of mine who'd been living in Ethiopia and went home to Edinburgh. 'Haven't seen you for a while,' said the barber, cutting his hair. 'I've been in Ethiopia,' said my friend. 'Oh aye,' said the barber. 'Is that on the number 24 bus route from Princes Street?'

What I know is that everyone lives on their own planet in their own time zone and they don't pay close attention to yours. You might find this really depressing, especially if you're under the illusion that you're very important and indispensable. I find it really liberating and useful. It means you can go somewhere and come back and the world won't have crumbled without you.

The way I see it is that we leave little ghostly selves all over the place. People take their memory of you and slot it into their virtual life. 'Has it really been six months?' they say. 'Doesn't time fly?' People sometimes say to me, 'You've been really busy lately, I've been seeing your name everywhere,' when what they've seen is my name in an old magazine they picked up in the dentist's waiting-room. I know not everyone leaves their name lying around in print, but risk taking off and see. If you take that sabbatical, do that round-the-world trip, you'll find your world doesn't come to an end. It will just get bigger, more elastic and a lot more interesting.

There is a looking-glass version of this idea. I know a jet-setting conductor who has just decided that the art of living is to do as much as possible without leaving home. In his case that means fewer tours of Japan and Europe and more time writing music and making recordings. So we can't all record music that puts our name out there, but when the world is linked by the internet we can send our ghostly self out into the world and allow our real self to dig the garden.

Whichever way you want to do it, you can lead more than one life at once.

Losing Control

You never know if you are learning something that might actually save your life.

I had been sent off to write an article on a day's rally for Porsche drivers at the Formula One racetrack at Brand's Hatch. Everyone there except me owned a Porsche (and some a Ferrari as well) and I was lent one, bright red. Top racing drivers took us out to practise slaloms and to cruise the track before anyone was allowed to let loose their Porsche round a world-class racetrack all by themselves.

Of course I was nervous, but first I went out in the passenger seat with one of Porsche's top drivers to pick up a few tips. It's scary going round a racetrack at high speed and it didn't help my nerves when the driver in front of us hit a bend too fast, lost control of the car and spun 180 degrees to end up on the grass verge facing the oncoming traffic.

'What she did wrong,' explained my driver calmly, 'was to brake hard when she felt the rear of her car drifting out on the bend. If she'd taken her hands and feet off the controls, the car would have corrected itself.'

'Yes, yes,' I said, earnestly making a mental note of everything he said.

Then it was my turn. I tootled off down the track, thinking how fast everything feels when you're so near the ground. I hit a bend. I felt the car swerve. I forgot everything I'd been told in an instinctive effort to slow the car down and I braked hard. The very expensive piece of machinery I was driving, which didn't belong to me, went out of my control, spun very fast in a screech of brakes and a cloud of dust and rubber and ended up on the verge facing in the wrong direction. Very shame-faced and embarrassed, I restarted the engine and crawled sedately back to the start. That was the end of my driving that day.

Fast forward 10 years. I am driving along a very crowded motorway in a large Peugeot estate car which is taking me and four children on a week's holiday. I pull routinely into the middle lane to overtake a very long European truck with an Austrian registration plate. As I drive alongside it there is a huge bang and suddenly I can't see anything at all out of the windscreen. The car is spinning uncontrollably at very high speed. Four children are screaming. Everything is a blur and I know quite clearly that this is it, this is the moment when I am going to die. At any moment I expect the shell of metal and glass around us to explode and shatter. The end.

In this very brief moment of thought I remember the time I was in a car spinning out of control before. This time I remember that in this extreme moment there is nothing I can do. I must not attempt to control the car in any way. I must let it right itself if it can. I relax my grip on the wheel and take my feet off the controls and wait, as the spinning and banging continue.

The car doesn't explode. Suddenly I find I can see out of the windscreen and what I can see is the crash barrier at the side of the road coming up rather fast at an angle of 45 degrees. This time I know I can brake and steer and all at once I am pulling up on the hard shoulder, straightening up, slowing down and stopping. I turn and look at the row of white faces behind me, expecting the side of the car to be stove in, dreading to see injury. Everyone is safe. We have been hit amidships by a juggernaut and we have survived.

I was vibrating with amazement and gratitude for days. Gratitude for being alive, gratitude for the children being alive. And one thing for which I was – am – hugely grateful was that I had a piece of experience in my armoury and it had worked.

But that experience, which I will never forget, taught me more than a way to drive my car. It taught me that sometimes the right thing to do in an extreme situation is to stop trying to control it.

When we get hit by shock and crisis it is natural to want to take charge, to do something. Sometimes this works. Sometimes it doesn't. Sometimes to do something out of reactive fear and panic makes things worse. Sometimes it's better to take a deep breath and ride out the shock waves. The situation isn't clear yet. It might not have played itself out. If you take your feet off the controls and coast – in a state of alertness – it can be very clear when the right moment to take action comes along.

Doing nothing is very difficult, but sometimes it is the only wise choice.

The Joy of Curfew

Twice in my life I've lived under curfew and I've loved it. Once was in Ethiopia, in a year of Marxist revolution. Nobody was allowed out on the roads after dark. Everyone had to stay in their own homes, or whichever home they happened to be in when curfew fell. Only the army and the police were allowed out on the streets, ready to catch any miscreant who happened to be out after dark.

The same thing happened in Afghanistan, three years later, after the Russian-backed coup of 1978. The cut-off was sunset and that was the end of driving out to see friends, eating dinner in restaurants, rehearsing plays, going to parties.

I was living in both countries with my husband, a doctor who was working for Save the Children Fund. Maybe being young, in love and happy with each other's company helped, but we still have a nostalgia for those confined, domestic nights. We spent them reading our way through the longest novels we could find. We got through the whole of Dickens and the whole of Trollope and we were saving up the great Russian novelists for our next posting and our next revolution.

Curfew is an extreme state imposed in conditions of extreme civil unrest and it imposes rules at the expense of civil liberties. But I also learned it had another side. Curfew wasn't just a cruel confinement, it was also a liberation. It was a liberation from restlessness, a liberation from the dissatisfaction of constantly feeling you could be having more fun somewhere else. It was a liberation from the subtle pressure to do the 101 things you do because you ought to, not necessarily because you want to. It was a liberation from the pressure to stay up late to show you were enjoying yourself and a passport to the pleasure of conversation and early nights without anyone thinking you were a party pooper.

There is a joy in constraint and a great spur to creativity. 'Total freedom,' said the composer Stravinsky 'is total inhibition.'

The removal of all boundaries often leads to inertia and inactivity. I have lived all my working life to deadlines, so much so that I find it hard to complete anything without them. Curfews, deadlines, budgets, briefs – the more restrictive they are, the more reassurance they can paradoxically bring.

A peacefulness descends on people who are restrained – the peacefulness of the wayward teenager who's finally been grounded, the driver whose car has broken down, the peacefulness there used to be on a Sunday when every shop was closed and the trains slowed down. Now everything is open and everyone is in their cars, off to spend money and have fun. Total freedom is total gridlock.

It is much easier if you have curfew, deadline and constraint imposed upon you, but you can do it yourself if you want to. Or, if you don't trust yourself to keep your own rules, take yourself off on a retreat where rules will be imposed on you. Even grown ups can bloom and relax when choice is taken away from them and calm order put in its place.

Practise Gratitude

There are two regular practices which can transform your attitude to and experience of life. One is gratitude. The other is forgiveness. They are the housekeeping tools of the mind and heart. One can fill you with a sense of the richness of life. The other cleans the dark and destructive corners of resentment, anger and hurt that accumulate, sometimes on a daily basis. If you are really down it can be difficult to practise either, but it is probably easier to switch your focus to gratitude than it is to forgive people who are hurting you.

Gratitude is always a good place to start from in the middle of turmoil. It is like a light which you can carry at will from the good places in your life to the dark places. It will illuminate them.

Gratitude begins as an instinctive, unfettered and free-flowing response to the good moments in life. When we are children it begins as a sense of awe and love, before we are taught to say 'thank you'. Then we sometimes find ourselves being made to say 'thank you', politely, for things we are not at all grateful for, so the sensation and the state get muddled. But you can find gratitude again. Remember the experience of receiving a spoonful of delicious ice cream, a sip of complex wine, an eyeful of moonlight, the sight of the sea, a tender touch, a helping hand, or the clean embrace of your own bed, whether it contains a teddy bear, a lover or simply rest at the end of a long and tiring day. Gratitude, unforced, will overwhelm you.

Remember those moments when you are in a beautiful place, in beautiful light, in beautiful weather, and all the goodness of the world seems to be spread unstintingly before you. You know, in every cell of your body, that it is sensational to be alive. Your whole self expands to receive your good fortune.

Remember those moments when you can hardly believe your luck. You have met someone wonderful who, miraculously, seems to think you are wonderful too. Or you find yourself in the heart of a group of friends, sustained by cheerfulness and good humour, and you think how lucky you are to have them. You lose a child in the supermarket and after a heart-stopping minute you find them again. That is gratitude.

Remember those moments when you are part of a crowd enjoying an extraordinary experience. Your team is scoring a winning goal. You are watching a great performance of an exciting play. At a concert, you are all on your feet, moving in time with the music. You will never forget it. You are so lucky to be here.

Narrow your focus. Remember the time you had a cold and somebody made you a hot drink. Remember the time you were stranded and somebody offered you a timely lift. Remember when the money to pay a debt came just in time. Remember the stranger who helped you carry a heavy bag up the stairs. These are simple everyday things, but they connect you with the flow of the world.

Everyone knows what gratitude is, what the sensation feels like. The trick in the conscious practice of gratitude is to reach into this emotional store and be grateful on purpose.

In moments of stress and depression it is far easier to follow a damaging practice of ingratitude, resentment, rage and blame. But these obsessive, negative thoughts switch on the chemicals in our bodies which damage our immune system and lead to states of depression and despair. The focus switches from the simple things we have to the innumerable things we don't have, even though others do. Ironically, the more we have, the more we want. But wise people, from the Buddha to the sociologists who have identified a modern sickness of luxury envy, know that want and desire can never be satisfied. The things we think we want are actually the source of our unhappiness.

The trick is to identify this pattern of thought and change it as soon as it occurs. Reach into your store at moments of trial and despair and apply the transformative balm of gratitude to your open wounds.

It seems impossible. You have real problems. Of course you have, but they won't be any easier to solve if you only focus on the damage they are doing to you. Negativity, self-pity, complaints are addictive, easy and irresistible. They darken vision so that hope and goodness are invisible. They are also a habit.

I have found that if I practise the habit of gratitude instead, starting with the smallest thing (and nothing is too small), my attitude can be swiftly transformed. I like the practice of Mother Teresa, who treated everything that came to her as a gift. 'Excuse me, Mother Teresa,' said one of her nuns when they faced a long weary delay at an airport, 'we have the gift of several hours' wait.' Advanced practitioners of gratitude can look on everything that happens to them – sickness, accident, bereavement, poverty – as a gift. They are the people who look back at a disaster and say, 'Oddly enough, that was one of the best things that ever happened to me.'

If you really want to feel enormous gratitude for your messy, problematic life, try nearly losing it. I have never felt so abundantly, humbly, unstintingly grateful, so in love with my life, as I did immediately after surviving a car crash. If your problems aren't life-threatening you can change your attitude to them by practising gratitude for the smallest things. And the moment to do this is when you find yourself feeling least grateful. Stop right there and say the simple words *thank you*.

Forgiveness

I would be a hypocrite if I said I found this easy. I just know that, along with the practice of conscious gratitude, forgiveness is the most important step you can take towards peace of mind and emotional freedom.

Life offers us innumerable opportunities to practise resentment, nurture hurt, replay grievance, simmer with justified anger, burn with betrayal. These strong emotions can consume us utterly. There have been times in my life when somebody has hurt me and in my constant replayings of the drama I have been the wronged one and they have been anywhere on the villainous scale from incomprehensible to downright cruel. If you think of yourself as a nice person, you simply long for others to repent of their evil ways and see things your way. If you aren't troubled by being nice, you may just want to kill them.

I've learned that the only way to survive with grace is to forgive. Nobody is hurt by your pain and anger but you, and the more you repeat the pain within yourself, the more damage is done. Take appropriate action by all means – this isn't about being a passive victim. Decide what results you would like. Make your feelings known, write a letter of complaint, even put the matter in the hands of the lawyers if you must, but emotionally let it go. There's no victory if you win your day in court and still feel bitter.

Of course you will find it hard, even impossible, to do this at first. The shock and hurt of being a victim can last a very long time, even a lifetime, and simply saying words of forgiveness will have no immediate emotional impact on you at all. If there is deep and lasting damage you may find relief and support in professional therapy. But if you begin the practice of forgiveness, it has the power of the drip of water that wears away the stone.

My friend Gloria Karpinski taught me an inner ritual of forgiveness. Imagine an altar of light. Imagine putting the person you need to forgive on this altar of light. Say, 'I forgive X for all sins against me, real or imaginary, in this life or any other.' Imagine the person dissolving in the light. Then place yourself on the altar and say, 'I forgive myself for all sins against X, whether real or imaginary, in this life or any other.' Or the words of the Lord's Prayer may be enough for you, if you reawaken their meaning: 'Forgive us our trespasses, as we forgive those that trespass against us.' Whatever our spiritual tradition, forgiveness is demanded of all of us.

We can practise forgiveness on a daily basis because we are injured on a daily basis, even in small ways. When somebody cuts you up in traffic, enrages you over the telephone or is rude in a shop, don't fume, don't seek to hurt back.

Above all, don't escalate and reproduce the hurt. Imagine surrounding the person with light and mentally say, 'I forgive and release you.' Even imagine blowing them a kiss – lightening this up with humour is a very good idea. And move on.

Without forgiveness I can tell you what happens. It is not the unforgiven who suffers. It is the person who can't forgive who carries the wrong, the hurt, the injury unhealed and constantly reactivated. That person is the one whose mind and body are in danger of being permanently damaged by pain, bitterness and resentment. Life is too short to suffer and be held by the past in this way. The practice of forgiveness, even when the wrongdoer continues to do wrong, is the only way to freedom and peace.

Write It Down

I write everything down. Shopping lists. 'To do' lists. Options. Projects. I couldn't travel anywhere without a notebook and I couldn't sleep without a diary. I've kept a diary for so long now that if I go too many days without unloading my thoughts and preoccupations into its pages I get an uneasy muddled feeling in my head. Writing everything down brings me clarity.

I don't write for anyone else, I write for myself, and my diaries make very boring reading. I don't write about world events or formulate great thoughts. I don't jot down the kind of material detail or social observation that would be useful to future historians. I use a diary to keep a record of my private and family life and, above all, to catch and clarify my feelings. And in formalizing my interior world on paper I gain some kind of control and perspective.

Above all, my diary is a place where I tell the truth to myself and record it. Because it is a journal of personal record, it's very useful for dispelling my own delusions and rewritings of my own history. I can look back several years and see what I really thought, not what I now think I thought. This can be humbling. I remember looking back several years once and realizing, to my shame, that the same boring things preoccupied me 10 years ago that preoccupy me now, that the same resolutions were constantly made and constantly and quickly broken. I still fret about going to the gym more, losing weight, working harder, using my talents better. I remember, on that day, feeling a simultaneous exasperation and relief at the absurdity of my own behaviour. I gave myself a holiday from pitiless self-flagellation and that New Year I deliberately didn't make any resolutions. I didn't get any fitter or lighter physically, but I did lighten up mentally and emotionally. I found a freedom in tolerant self-acceptance.

Once you have the notebook and diary habit you are building your own reference book, your guide to your own life. It's a record of what you really did, how you really felt. It can be full of useful clues and reminders, a repository of insights and ideas. It's a record of people you met, ambitions you had, circumstances in which you were excited and happy, bored or sad. Maybe you can create new happiness from the clues you left yourself. And as for the circumstances in which you constantly make yourself miserable, your diary provides the information you need to recognize them and step aside.

Above all, a diary is a way to debrief yourself of a day in your life so that your mind is unloaded and ready for sleep. My friend Gloria Karpinski has a nice prayer for the end of the day. It begins, 'I release the fullness of this day…' I like that. When I say it I recognize that even the most unmemorable day is actually full of detail once you begin to replay it in your head or write it down. Often it is in the act of writing itself that the significance is revealed. Or you might be so full of the emotion of a memorable day that the act of writing is purging.

You don't have to re-read what you have written for it to have value, though re-reading at a later date – a year, five years, ten years on – might surprise you. I re-read my diary at the end of a year and try to make sense of my own experience. How far have I travelled? What worked and what didn't? What did I start and abandon? What ideas were never developed? What new friendships did I make? What old ones did I nurture? What did I learn that I can carry forward? How can I build a new year on the old one?

Keeping a diary is a habit rather than a discipline. Once it has gripped you, it becomes a necessary part of a self-maintenance programme, like brushing your hair or cleaning your teeth. Only it isn't your body you are maintaining (though a record of your physical health can be very useful): you are providing a log book for your heart and soul.

Live Life on Approval

Disapproval is bad for you. It sours your heart and turns the corners of your mouth down. Justified complaint, thoroughly pursued, is one thing. A constant nagging sense of irritation is another. It means giving house room to a doom-laden inner monologue:

> *The train service is hopeless. What does that girl think she looks like? Why can't you get a decent cup of coffee round here? Why do people shout when they're on their mobile phone? Litter lout! Get out of my way! You might not be in a hurry, but I am.*

What's not to get annoyed about? Check your expression, though, and the state of your blood pressure. You may be in the right, but do you want to end up looking like a hypertensive prune?

I've noticed that our culture encourages criticism, not celebration. It's cool not to be fooled. I've also noticed that it feels much better to be delighted than depressed, and it's certainly more energizing to rave than to rant, to open up than to close off.

I have a trick I use when I catch myself out in a monologue of disapproval: I approve, on purpose. I start consciously looking for things to praise. Absolutely anything will do to turn the tide. I'm walking along the street cursing the kids who are blocking the way, the loud radio playing from a window, the high speed of that motorbike. Stop, stop. My disapproval only hurts me. I approve of the bright colour they've painted that door. I approve of the way that man slowed his car down for me to cross the road. I approve of the pink flower that shop assistant is wearing in her hair. I approve of the way that workman is whistling as he waits for the bus. In fact, the more I look at this street, the more there is to approve of. My heart is lighter and the set of my mouth has changed.

Approval feels better. It's healthier. And if I want to magnify the good feeling, I've learned that it really works to pass the approval on. I sat next to an African woman on the bus home. She was wearing a wonderful blue robe and turban. She looked so good I kept looking at her sideways and the thought grew on me that I really ought to pass my approval on. I'm quite a reserved person, but I finally took a risk. In my polite English way I said, 'I hope you don't mind my saying this, but I think you look fabulous.' Her face lit up with an enormous smile. 'Why, *thank you*,' she said, beaming. So that made two people enjoying the effects of approval.

Approval changes the filter of your day. It lifts your mood, multiplies your appreciation of life and, when you pass it on, that's cheerfulness squared.

Torture Yourself

Sometimes it's good to torture yourself. I think I've always known it, but when I was told it by the distinguished orchestral conductor Sir Colin Davis, who takes a break from learning orchestral scores by knitting fiendishly complicated sweaters, I wrote it down.

I realize that people are torturing themselves around me all day. The men turning purple and dripping sweat onto the treadmills at the gym are torturing themselves. My mother doing her nightly crossword is torturing herself. My friend training for a marathon is torturing himself. My neighbour translating, unasked and unpaid, a Spanish novel into English is torturing himself.

I did it to myself when I decided to do a late Master's degree at the same time as earning a living. For two years I banged my head on brick walls of learning new skills and tackling difficult problems of my own making and I often wondered, out loud, why I was making life so impossible for myself. And yet I was quite proud of myself too. I knew that I had made a commitment to living, to growing, to stretching, to challenging myself. It hurt, and an easier, quieter existence wouldn't have done, but it wouldn't have felt like living either.

No pain, no gain applies to anything that's a stretch. Difficulty is good for us, which is why, when life becomes too soft, too boring, we are programmed to seek it out. And difficulty overcome is like a blood transfusion. I remember knowing, as I neared the end of my MA, that now I'd worked this hard and tortured myself this effectively, nothing would ever be this much of a struggle again.

My Head is a Free Space

I say, 'My head is a free space.' I imagine a border shutting, dividing the free territory of my head from the clamouring crowd of refugee thoughts that would like to come in. Outside the border post are the hordes of critical voices, negative thoughts, corrosive doubts. They clamour. They shout. They press forward, waving their passports, their claims to residency – after all, they're used to coming and going as they please. But they can't come in now. My head is a free space.

I suddenly feel clear and light. Nothing – no thought, no comment – enters unless I allow it. I choose to exclude all the illegal immigrants of the mind, all the armies of guilt and fear that undermine my ability to act. As I imagine the free state of my head, I can see the invading thoughts for what they are – a demoralizing army which destroys my happiness, my confidence, my ability to think clearly and consciously.

The feeling makes me realize I could choose my thoughts instead of having them choose me. Instead of worrying about that insurance claim I could choose to plan a summer holiday or replay a happy family lunch. I could recite a piece of poetry to myself, hum a favourite tune, recall a special place and walk round it in my imagination. Imagination is salvation.

Yet, because demoralizing thoughts and repetitive ideas are used to occupying my head and because I am very used to entertaining them, it is very easy for them to slip past my defences. Before I know it, I am invaded again. But each time this happens I am aware of it sooner. I act more quickly. I recite my mantra and expel them. 'My head is a free space.' I really don't want this replaying of an office argument, this rehearsing of a complaint, this mental rewriting of a letter to someone who's let me down. So out with them. 'My head is a free space,' I say sharply, and the bad thoughts run for the border.

This is an emergency measure, something effective and simple to do when I realize I'm being driven by thoughts. But it requires that I notice my own thought processes first. Most of us are so habitual in our thinking – so *unthinking*, in fact – that we don't even notice what it is we think about, let alone realize that we have any choice about what goes on in our own heads.

Try this. Try saying 'My head is a free space' at regular intervals and notice what runs for cover.

Fleeting Feelings

In my experience, if you are in the grip of a very strong emotion it is impossible to think or act straight. Better not to try, but then how do you deal with the emotion?

Once in my life I experienced paralysing fear and I found the antidote and it worked. It was an internal fear, by the way. I wasn't in any immediate physical danger or in a situation where I had to think fast, which was just as well, because I wasn't able to think at all.

The house where I lived at the time had bad subsidence and I was involved in a big insurance claim. One morning I took a phone call which left me thinking that everything was going to fall through. The insurance company wasn't going to pay up. The house was going to fall down. I had no money to do the work. My house would be uninhabitable and unsaleable and I would be broke. The vision of my future that suddenly filled me was terrifying – homeless, in debt, trapped. I was a frozen cliché. I was so paralysed by sheer survival fear that I could hardly breathe.

It was then, as I stood immobile by my phone, that I remembered an antidote. I had been reading a book by the Vietnamese Buddhist monk Thich Nhat Hanh. He was writing about the Buddhist approach to emotions as forces that worked though you like a weather system. His recommendation for paralysing moments like mine was to identify the feeling – fear, no question – and gently to repeat this mantra: 'Feelings of fear are passing through me.'

I stood there by the phone and took a few deep breaths, then I began. 'Feelings of fear,' I told myself, 'are passing through me. Feelings of fear are passing through me. Feelings of fear are passing through me.' The effect wasn't instant, but it was slowly noticeable. It took perhaps 10, 15 minutes of repetition, anguished at first, then slowly calmer, for the words to take effect.

What happened was that gradually a gap formed between the over-whelming feelings and whatever 'I' was, an entity that observed and was there before the feelings and would be there after them. The feelings, overpowering as they were, were not swallowing me up. I was surviving them. I found myself straightening up and walking away. The moment of emergency had passed. And I knew what to do if it struck again, which it never did in quite the same way.

The mantra gave me a vital sense of distance and control and it was gentle and rational, much kinder than the impatient voice we too often use which goes, 'Don't be so stupid. Pull yourself together. Stop being a baby.' The Buddhist voice acknowledges reality and reminds us that it is fleeting. No emotion lasts forever.

Incidentally, the insurance problem was solved and I moved house. The day before I moved I found the perfect antidote to the inevitable stress and disorder. I left my packing cases behind for a few hours and went to hear Thich Nhat Hanh talk in person. Like his books, he was the essence of calm and humane wisdom. My move went smoothly and a difficult phase of my life came to an end.

The Beauty Way

I first came across the Beauty Way of the Navajo in a book called *Find your Own North Star* by Martha Beck. It has been a constant resource for me ever since. I found that it has the power to transform my experience of the everyday, to shine the light of magic onto the most mundane, even ugly, surroundings. All that makes the Beauty Way one of the most extraordinary and powerful tools in my toolbox.

Here's how it works. I am stuck in my car in heavy traffic on a very unlovely through road in a semi-industrialized soulless corner of south London. My body is cramped and uncomfortable. My mind is resistant and very resentful. My heart is down. I try reciting the Beauty Way:

> *There is beauty above me.* High white clouds are racing across a deepening evening sky. Their form and motion and free flow remind me of the westerly winds that are carrying them over the city from the open spaces of the Atlantic Ocean, over the green hills of the West Country. They are beginning to catch the apricot warmth of the sinking sun. They draw my mind eastward, to the English Channel, the darkening fields of Belgium and northern France, even further east to the Russian mountains, where our icy east winds come from in winter.

There is beauty before me. The tail-lights of the van in front glow a rich fiery red. There is an abstract pattern in the flaking paint and rust. The dying sun is reflected in the tall glass wall of an office block ahead. Suddenly it stops being an ugly concrete block and becomes a stack of magic mirrors. The stalled traffic curves ahead, a serpentine line of smouldering red lights, to the traffic lights. Red – a rich luminous ruby. Amber – a warm, glowing orange. Green – an intense turquoise like the inside of an ice cave. Why hadn't I noticed how beautiful traffic lights were before? Everyday beauty, casually ignored.

There is beauty to the left of me. A quick glance (I am meant to be driving). The car in the next lane is a gleaming abstract of reflections, a dark gleam of high-gloss paintwork, a slick of mirror, a transparent bafflement of glass which requires two lengths of focus, one for the dazzling surface, one for the dark interior. Why have I never noticed what a complex, subtle, mysterious object a car is?

There is beauty to the right of me. To the right there is the same play of light on colours and reflective surfaces as the traffic streams past. As evening falls, a few headlights begin to shine, starlike, in the gleaming flow of metal and glass.

There is beauty below me. It's hard to look down in a car and I certainly can't do it while I'm driving, but the lights turn red again. My eyes are caught and fascinated by the folded fabric of my own clothes on my lap, the subtle textures, the little canyons of light and shade in the pleats and creases.

There is beauty behind me. A curving chain of lights is framed in my rearview mirror. The shape of the mirror itself miniaturizes and formalizes the abstraction of lights and tones, geometric shapes and subtle curves.

There is beauty all round me. Yes, there is. Thank you.

There is beauty inside me. There is. My anger and frustration have been transformed by the exercise of looking. What was a source of rage and impatience has become a source of fascination, pleasure and revelation. Of course I would much rather not be in a traffic jam and I don't want to arrive rushed and stressed at my destination, but my experience has been wholly altered. I feel I have been given a priceless gift: seeing the world as a constant source of magic. I am awake and grateful.

Seek and Ye Shall Find

Once upon a time I designed a ghost train. It was a dark ride through the ancient Underworld. The project took two years and when I'd finished it I'd earned a Master's degree in design and illustration. I must have been obeying my own advice to torture myself because over those two years I went to hell and back in all kinds of different and imaginative ways. I learned about fairground architecture, animation, Greek mythology, mask-making and street theatre, theatrical lighting, storyboarding, sound design, narrative structure and an awful lot about death and what people, ancient and modern, think happens to them when they die.

What I learned filled a whole project report and I won't bother you with it. But I learned one big thing: I learned that whatever you look for you will see. When you have an obsession, a project, an *idée fixe*, a world view, the world obligingly rearranges itself to suit you. I spent a lot of time thinking about ghost trains and the world kindly kept presenting me with ghost trains. My life became one giant coincidence. It wasn't simply as though I had permanent ghost train antennae on my head, though it was like that. It was as though I had a dirty great flashing neon sign saying: 'Interested in ghost trains. Come and get me.'

Here's one example. In the middle of preparing for my course I took a break and went for a walk in a nearby park. By the pond was a happy little crowd of elderly gentlemen sailing model boats and when I got up close I saw a sign saying 'Merton and District Society of Model Engineers'. My tutors at art college were always asking me when I was going to start making a model of my ghost train and I was always trying to change the subject. I didn't have a clue how to make a model. But here were some cheerful old gentlemen who obviously did have a clue. 'Do you know anybody,' I asked one of them, 'who could possibly give me a hand?' 'Funnily enough,' he said, 'our secretary won a prize last year for his working model of a ghost train.' Bingo! And likewise, 'Eureka!' The antennae worked again.

Seek and ye shall find. A coincidence is only a question meeting an answer in an unexpected way. There's nothing mystical about it and the clearer and more concise you are in your questions, the harder you work at it, the more quickly and exactly the world will give you a response. I met a girl in a restaurant the other day. She'd decided to buy a second-hand car and had e-mailed 12 people to tell them what she wanted and four had come right back at her with cars they knew about. All she had to do was choose.

The world will meet your expectations in a negative as well as a positive way. Very gloomy people who expect the worst of life are always satisfied. Their lives are, indeed, disappointing to them, even if they look quite satisfactory to other people. But if you spend time with the Eeyores of this world you realize they create life in their own image. Their antennae quiver with the daily proof they need that life is a dark and dangerous business. And what's more, they experience all the unhappiness of waiting for things to go wrong. Things do go wrong, of course, but I've noticed that cheerful people with high expectations of happiness don't waste much time worrying or grieving after the event. Much better to have a large flashing neon sign on your head which says: 'I'm interested in happiness. Come and get me.'

A Damn Good Listening To

A friend of mine was laughing at a phrase he'd heard in a monastery he'd visited. One of the monks was talking about another. 'What that man needs,' he said, 'is a damn good listening to.'

If there is anything we all need, it's a damn good listening to. The feeling of being truly heard is rare, flattering, calming, reassuring and completely wonderful. Simple attention defuses hurt and anger, relieves tension, and gives a strong message that the other person is worthwhile and important. It gives the space and the ground to resolve difficulties.

But pay attention to the people around you. Is listening going on? Or is there an awful lot of interrupting? Are you aware that most people keep an impatient silence while someone else is talking because they are only waiting for the right moment to jump in with their own ideas, their own experience. Are you aware that the unspoken (yet) words, 'Yes, but...' hover over most listeners' heads? That is, if they are listening at all. They could be, and often are, thinking about something completely different.

The feeling of not being listened to can have explosive results. I once threw plates at someone who wasn't listening to me. Or it can lead to terrible depressions. Someone who isn't heard can quickly feel that there is no point in speaking, that they don't exist at all.

The feeling of being listened to can be just as powerful. Giving someone a good listening to can heal sickness and change relationships. I learned this when my children were teenagers and I came across a book called *How to Talk So Kids Will Listen and Listen So Kids Will Talk* by Adele Faber and Elaine Mazlish. It made a real difference to communication in our house. I was chastened to realize how much of what I thought was friendly conversation came across as inquisition. I learned how the barrage of questions I greeted my children with at the end of the school day sounded like a loaded interrogation to them. I learned that if I kept quiet or burbled about something inconsequential, they would unravel or raise things at their own pace. I learned, and I never stop learning, to bite my tongue. I learned that one secret of successful communication is simply to pay subtle attention, so that you notice when the important things are being said. This isn't an easy thing to do, especially when all of us are so full of answers and good advice. It's something I keep learning.

I had a conversation with one of my children the other day. She was anxious to quit her job. I was more than anxious about how she was going to pay her bills. I was so full of things I wanted to say to her that I was halfway through another useful piece of advice before I realized that what she'd just said was, 'Do you want to know what I really want to do with my life?' With a mental screech of brakes I managed to shut up in time to say, 'Yes, please tell me what you really want to do with your life.' And she told me.

Listening to people is much harder when you are dying to get your own point of view across, and harder still when you are emotional, whether you are angry, aggrieved, hurt or even distraught. That is why so many situations need mediators. If you need to talk about something difficult and emotional with another person and you don't want to use a mediator or facilitator, it is worth trying to agree some boundaries while you are both calm. It works if you agree on a set time during which each person can speak, uninterrupted, and say what they need to say. It also works if you allow for a pause, and if each person agrees to repeat back what they think they've heard before they say their piece.

Giving people a damn good listening to is so important that it's worth consciously practising your listening skills. Just tell yourself that for the next hour, the next day, you will listen to everyone you meet without interrupting, advising or judging. You may learn things you didn't know. You will definitely feel much less stressed.

Integrate or Disintegrate

What if you get what you wish for? Will you live happily ever after? Or will you just have created a job vacancy for another wish?

My friend and teacher Gloria Karpinski has a good nugget of wisdom: Don't lust for more than you can integrate. This doesn't mean you can't have big dreams and ambitions, just that you should be aware of the line between desire and greed. This is such a good idea. When I heard it I thought it was meant for me. I have spent a lifetime with my eyes bigger than my stomach. The result of this, alas, is that your stomach ends up being a whole lot bigger than your eyes. Lusting after more than you can integrate has a lot of other direct and visible consequences. You have a cupboard full of once irresistible clothes that you hardly ever wear. Think of Imelda Marcos's shoes.

Or you fill a diary with dates. It makes you feel loved and wanted, but beware being the type of person who always cancels at the last minute, or who arrives perpetually late, perpetually rushed, because you're trying to cram in one more undigested, unexperienced experience. When friends begin to feel just squeezed into someone's life they eventually squeeze themselves right out again. A friendship that isn't integrated soon disintegrates.

Perhaps, like me, you have a serious book habit. The painter who had to shift hundreds of books to get at my walls said, 'Have you really read all these?' 'Oh yes,' I said, exaggerating a bit. What about the piles of books by my bed? If they were apples they'd all have a couple of bites taken out of them and lie in a rotting heap. Books don't do that. They just lie there patiently gathering dust until I decide to take another bite from one of them. The rot is in the effect they have on my energy, the way they silt up my space. I think back to when I bought each one. The inviting pile of new books in the bookstore. Only a few pounds each. Educational. Good for the soul. I was brought up to equate books with virtue, so an impulse buy is easy to justify. But back home it soon goes on the pile. And unintegrated books just mean more to dust.

And what about the evening classes which are going to change your life, abandoned on the first wet winter night? The correspondence course uncompleted. The miraculous beauty creams half-used in the jar. The exercise machine gathering dust in the spare bedroom. The sailing boat that never leaves the boatyard. The gym membership that's unused after six weeks. Never forget that Mr Colman of Colman's Mustard once said he'd made his fortune from the mustard that people left on the side of their plates.

Why does this matter? Because it's all a waste – a waste of money, a waste of whatever it is you spent the money on – and because it's the visible evidence of a huge failure of self-discipline and self-knowledge. And because the detritus, the clutter unintegrated possessions make, is so depressing. It clogs up the emotional arteries of our lives as well as our cupboards.

What I did that worked, in terms of curbing the lust for more than I can integrate, was to buy a fairly small wardrobe and never have more clothes than could comfortably hang in it. It would be a good idea to do the same with bookcases.

I don't think that I, or most of us who aren't monks or nuns, will ever quite crack this one because we all live in a society where happiness is identified with acquisition. But I've learned to ask not 'Do I want this?' but 'Do I really, really, want this? Where am I going to put it? Am I ever going to use it?' I've learned that what I don't integrate disintegrates, and with it, some of my bank balance, my energy, my sense of order and my peace of mind.

Looking Up

This is very simple. Look up more. All sad emotional states express themselves with hunched shoulders, downcast eyes, closed-in postures. Downheaded is downhearted. Don't be downhearted. Look up and be uplifted.

If you look up, you will expand your world. You will see clouds, weather, the colour of the sky, the stars and planets, the flight of birds, the pattern of branches, the silver trail of planes. If you look up, you'll notice all the creative, expressive, witty, quirky things that architects, builders, sculptors do that nobody notices. You'll see gargoyles and flags, the gleaming top of the Chrysler Building, the wisp of cloud that streams from Canary Wharf, the lights on the Eiffel Tower. You'll see the sky reflected in a million windows. You'll see sculptures and mottos and coats of arms, ceiling mouldings and classical friezes, angels and cherubs. You'll see kites and balloons and aerial messages, giant cranes and skyscrapers. Lift up your eyes and you will see hills and horizons, the skein of winter geese, the first swallow of summer.

And yet everyone trudges along, their eyes on the ground or no higher than the next human being.

Freedom is overhead. Look up and you will feel different. Apart from anything else, looking up is a very effective way of stopping yourself crying!

Speak in Tongues

If you want your world to expand gloriously, your life to become rich, exotic, full of new discovery, pleasure and understanding, learn another language.

It is little credit to me that I have two languages, English and French. I owe it to my teachers at school, to my parents, who arranged for me to spend my holidays with a family in France, and above all to the Famille Guieu, who gave me a double life and who are still my friends and family, with who knows what pleasures still to come as we keep visiting and talking to each other.

Learning another language isn't simply a matter of cramming vocabulary, struggling with irregular verbs and being baffled by sentence structure. It's the discovery of a completely different world view which shows you better than any theory can that your way of thinking and being is not the only way, nor the best.

Even the effort made to learn a small holiday vocabulary yields rewards – smiles, chance encounters and good will. Taking the trouble to say 'please' and 'thank you' in a foreign language is the minimum courtesy travellers can offer and yet all over the world I hear people from English-speaking countries sticking firmly, loudly and sometimes arrogantly to their native tongue. We're the ones missing out.

With a smattering of a language, the world beyond your borders becomes a joyous game. There is something primally satisfying about unravelling a code. I once took a two-week fast-track course in Greek and followed it with a two-week holiday in the Pelepponese. I did it because I love Greece and I was fed up with being tongue-tied there. My joy at being able to call the plumber to fix a leaking lavatory and to explain to a car mechanic how my car needed help was equal to deciphering a line of Homer.

One thing about languages: if you don't use them, you lose them. They can only be imprinted in the labyrinth of your brain through repetition. I'm out of practice and I couldn't talk to a Greek plumber any more, but I can decipher road signs and newspaper headlines. I love hearing Greek parents address their babies as Aristotle and Odysseus. I love knowing that the Greeks invented the language of the heart and mind, nostalgia and philosophy, tragedy and psychology. I love the little window in the mind that opens when you learn that the Greek word for 'single' is the same as the word for 'free'.

The joy of learning another language is that there is rarely a direct translation. Whole realms of philosophy are opened up by learning that whole words, whole concepts, are missing in another national brain.

And worlds are open to you. My French has taken me in and out of love with French boys, round the Elysée Palace with Madame Mitterrand, through a Berber village with an old peasant in the High Atlas in Morocco and into drinking disastrous amounts of *eau de vie* with French farmers in the Lot Valley.

Learning a language, just for its own sake, can even take your life in a whole new direction. In her first year at university my friend Susie decided to take Farsi classes at university, on a whim. She got hooked. She changed her degree from anthropology to Farsi. She spent six months studying in Iran. She found temporary volunteer work at a human rights agency. September 11th happened and Susie, the only Farsi speaker in the office, found herself dealing directly with people in Afghanistan, where they speak Dari, a close relation of Farsi. A year later she was working in Kabul, an experience which was difficult, but valuable and unforgettable.

I can't promise that if you start evening classes in Spanish or Serbo-Croat something like this will happen to you. But I do know that learning another language could lead to experiences, pleasures, encounters and possibilities you can't even dream of.

Running Away Money

My Great Aunt Kate always told her three daughters that they had to have running away money, especially once they got married. She was ahead of her time, but then she knew something about running away money herself, as she'd run away from her marriage once or twice in her younger days, even though she kept going home again.

My Great Aunt Kate grew up at a time when it was unusual for women to have their own money, but she knew that running away money was leverage. It made all the difference between enduring what life threw at you, particularly an unhappy marriage, and having the means to get out and live life on your own terms. When it comes to buying a bit of freedom and a degree of control over your own destiny, running away money is a gender-free zone.

Everyone should have running away money. I'll give it another name. Everyone should have savings. I sing the joy, the liberation, the comfort and protection of savings, from the glorious pile of coins collected from benign aunts and uncles that I saved in my pink plastic piggy bank with the blue cap to the savings accounts that have several times given me breathing space between commissions and contracts, even bought me whole years off and the freedom to travel or just say 'no'.

Running away money means not having to panic if things go wrong. Running away money means you could do that course or take that trip. Running away money means you can take a sabbatical, a gap year, a career break. Running away money means you need never be anybody's slave, not in a job, not in a family, not in a relationship.

It was running away money that freed me to go and live in Africa for 18 months. It was running away money that meant, when a life coach wondered if I could afford to stop working and re-evaluate for three months, that I could, and the feeling of liberation was fantastic. It was running away money that meant I could make the same decision for myself a few years down the line and go to art school.

Savings are unfashionable. Debt is fashionable. Few things enrage me more than the cynical way in which financial institutions suck people into debt as soon as they are old enough to have a bank account. 'You can't afford to pay off your loan? Then we didn't lend you enough. Here, have an even bigger loan.' For 'loan' read 'debt'.

Your body can tell the difference. Debts and loans, after the brief initial rush of having some money in your hand, produce a sinking, fearful feeling in the pit of your stomach. They haunt you. Knowing you have savings somewhere makes you feel light and calm.

How do you get that feeling? I know how many young people are saddled with debts and student loans at the very start of their working lives, but you can still save. Saving is a habit and savings accumulate. One drink less here, a walk to work there, a homemade sandwich instead of the café, a night in with a video rather than a night out at a restaurant. It adds up. And, unlike taking out loans, saving money regularly adds enormously to your feelings of self-control and self-worth. Even saving small change on a regular basis can accumulate enough money for a holiday or celebration. The important thing is to get the habit.

Sing and the World Sings with You

This is personal to me, but there is an equivalent for you. I joined a choir and it changed my life. I'd say more: I joined a choir and it *saved* my life.

It happened this way. When I was at school we had a charismatic music teacher called Dr Moore Morgan. Twice a year, in spring and summer, Dr Morgan somehow galvanized half the school into joining his choir and tackling great music. Mozart's *Requiem. The Magic Flute*. Haydn's Creation. Mendelssohn's *Elijah*. Most of us learned it all by ear because we couldn't sight-read and that was when I first learned what it felt like to be possessed by music.

I left school and was swept away by rock and pop and I danced a lot but I didn't sing any more. When my forties rolled around I began to feel a longing to sing in a choir again. Through my door came a letter from the music teacher at my children's school. He was thinking of starting a parents' choir, no sight-reading required, everyone welcome. A week later I was there, getting my vocal chords round Bach's *Christmas Oratorio* and feeling alive again. Within two years, after regular singing lessons with the same teacher, I could sight-read well enough to audition for the London Symphony Chorus.

One of the first concerts I sang in, with the London Symphony Orchestra, was *Candide*, conducted by Leonard Bernstein. As we rehearsed in the Barbican with Bernstein and a glittery cast of star singers I had a second of alert awareness when I knew I wasn't in Kansas any more. My home life and my emotional life at the time were bleak. My marriage was breaking up and I was at a very low point, but in those rehearsals and performances of *Candide* another door opened for me and I entered a different world – heightened, imaginative, glorious. I really wasn't in Kansas any more. My membership of the chorus was a passport to Oz.

In fact, singing anywhere – in the bath, in church, in a choir, in a football crowd – is a passport to Oz. It's a physical, emotional and spiritual release, and if you are singing the great classical repertoire, it is a huge mental challenge too.

Singing gives expression to feelings. It produces endorphins, shakes tension out of muscles and obsessions and repetitive thoughts out of brains. It opens hearts and brings exhilaration – literally, out-of-breathness. You have to breathe deeply to sing properly.

Singing in a choir is also social. If you work alone, as I do, or in a highly competitive and stressful work environment, it is a blessed release to become a small cog in a larger machine, a tiny part of a greater whole. You struggle in states of individual difficulty to master the music, but you experience sublime moments when the whole comes together and is united and transcendent.

Singing in a choir also brings the experience of selflessness. You're not a soloist. You are necessary, but your voice must blend in and you mustn't let your fellow choristers down. It is an act of self-gratification, but it is also an act of service. Egos aren't encouraged. Social standing and success beyond the rehearsal doors don't matter. Service to the music and mastery of it are the great levellers. The better the music you are working on, the greater the sense of duty to it and the privilege in being allowed to perform it. Dedication is required. There will be hours of rehearsal and yet, at the end of a hard day and a trying journey, those hours of rehearsal can be what made the day worthwhile.

And then there is the service of performance. If you are lucky enough to join a big choir you will have the joy of singing with an orchestra and skilled soloists and, if you're really lucky, a brilliant and inspiring conductor who can communicate the composer's intentions and raise the game of everyone on stage. From the moment the conductor raises his baton every individual on the concert platform is giving everything to do justice to the composer's intention and to deliver the experience of a lifetime to the audience whose pale faces fill the rows of seats. Few things are more gratifying than the explosion of cheers and applause at the end of a great performance, or, even more, the stillness of attention given by an audience that is moved and enthralled by what they are hearing.

Or you can experience singing quite differently. You can know the intimacy and tender connection that takes place when you sing a baby to sleep with a simple lullaby. Babies don't give a hoot whether you have a great singing voice or not, but they love the feeling of being rocked in song.

If you don't want to join a choir, you can still experience the joy of communal singing in classes and workshops. I've tried Georgian folk singing, overtone chanting, gospel singing and madrigals, jazz singing and musical theatre. There are even classes for people who think they can't sing. At every level I've seen the transformation and transfiguration that occur when people who start to sing insecurely and nervously open up and bloom. They have let the music in and experienced the release that occurs at every level when you become an instrument.

The great gospel singer Mahalia Jackson said that when she travelled round the States she liked to drop in at a local black church and just sing along with the congregation. She called these places her 'filling stations'. The London Symphony Chorus is one of my filling stations. There's one for you somewhere.

Calm Down

Does anything irritate you more than being told to calm down? It's an instant recipe for high blood pressure and enraged thoughts. But that doesn't stop it being a good idea.

I know one way to calm down which was taught me by a Chinese medical practitioner and chi gong teacher. I've forgotten everything else he taught me, but this has stuck and it is my best relaxation-during-the-day and getting-to-sleep-at-night technique, something I use several times a week.

Begin by sitting down, closing your eyes and focusing on your breathing. Actually, if you feel like doing this in a public place, you don't even have to close your eyes. Don't try and alter your breathing, but be aware of the subtle movements of your body as you take in air and breathe it out. Consciously relax your jaw, let your teeth part and let your tongue rest with its tip against the back of your lower teeth. Then take your attention to the crown of your head and begin this simple process.

Move your attention downwards as you recite the following words to yourself on the in breath. Breathe out and consciously release any tension on the out breath.

Mind to top of head: 'Top of head, relax.'
Mind to temples: 'Temples, relax.'
Mind to jaw: 'Jaw, relax.'
Mind to neck: 'Neck, relax.'
Mind to shoulders: 'Shoulders, relax.'
Mind to upper arms: 'Upper arms, relax.'
Mind to elbows: 'Elbows, relax.'
Mind to forearms: 'Forearms, relax.'
Mind to hands: 'Hands, relax.'

Rest for a few moments, remaining consciously aware of your breath. Then take your attention back to the crown of your head and begin the second round:

Mind to top of head: 'Top of head, relax.'
Mind to face: 'Face, relax.'
Mind to heart: 'Heart, relax.'
Mind to stomach: 'Stomach, relax.'
Mind to thighs: 'Thighs, relax.'
Mind to knees: 'Knees, relax.'
Mind to lower legs: 'Lower legs, relax.'

Mind to ankles: 'Ankles, relax.'
Mind to feet: 'Feet, relax.'

Then rest again.

If you want to, repeat the cycle.

You can do this anywhere, anytime. As well as calming you down, it will instantly lower your blood pressure.

Thinking Straight and Feeling Good

One day the editor I was working for told me to go and see a psychiatrist. It's one of the joys of journalism that when you wake up in the morning you have no idea what the day will bring, but this was more off-the-wall than usual. She didn't think I was mad, but she wanted me to pretend I was.

What had happened was that the Priory, the private hospital of choice for burnt-out rock stars and addicted celebrities, was opening a branch near the City of London, aiming to catch burnt-out bankers and addicted traders. 'Book yourself an appointment,' said my editor, 'and write about what it's like.'

It didn't take me more than two minutes to realize that any good psychiatrist was likely to rumble a faking journalist in very short order. If I was going to do this job at all I was going to have to find a way to be truthful, so I found myself sitting in front of a highly qualified psychiatrist telling him the truth, which was this: that I was a journalist, that the previous year I had suffered a period of clinical depression which had been treated with tranquillizers and that I had also seen a therapist. I was no longer seeing the therapist and I had stopped the pills after three months but the early symptoms of that depression – the disturbed sleep, gloomy thoughts and a feeling of dread in the pit of my stomach – were beginning to return. I didn't want to take any more medication, so did he have anything else to suggest and, by the way, did he know anything about cognitive behaviour therapy because I'd heard it was good?

It turned out that I had booked an appointment with one of the relatively few psychiatrists in Britain who was also a trained cognitive behaviour therapist. In his experience, he said, it was effective and suitable for everything except psychosis.

Cognitive behaviour therapy is very practical and, unlike any other form of psychotherapy, it puts the techniques for change directly into the hands of the patient. Its premise is that bad feelings come from illogical thinking and that once you can identify your faulty thinking, you can counteract it. This well-tried process of self-analysis and correction will make the bad feelings go away.

Controlled trials have shown cognitive behaviour therapy to be as effective as medication for depression, and more long-lasting. Unlike other forms of psychotherapy it is relatively quick to take effect. No years lying on the couch remembering how mean your parents were to you – cognitive behaviour therapy starts with how you feel and act right now this minute.

The nice psychiatrist offered me a few sessions to get started, which I didn't take because he also gave me the name of a book for the general reader, *Feeling Good: The New Mood Therapy* by Dr David D. Burns, based on his years of research at the University of Pennsylvania. I found the book in my local bookshop the same day and started doing the exercises in it, and that was all I ever needed.

I know exactly how depressed I was because one of the tools in the book is a depression index of questions which helps you grade yourself from mild to severe. If you are severely depressed – which, according to the index, means contemplating suicide and having worked out the means to do it – then please seek medical help. I was never that depressed, though I continued to use the book over the next couple of months until I realized I wasn't turning to it any more. It stays on my shelf as a valuable resource, even though I've not needed to use it again, and I recommend it to other people because, unlike many forms of therapy which often depend a great deal on the intuition, personality and skill of the therapist, cognitive behaviour therapy is extremely practical, structured and logical, and it works. If you prefer a person to a book, a search on the internet will find you your nearest cognitive behaviour therapist.

Flower Remedies

The first time I ever took a flower remedy was when I was soaking wet and shivering after a very cold day spent falling in and out of a Welsh mountain river. Somebody in the group produced a little brown bottle of something called Rescue Remedy and insisted that we prise open our chattering jaws and take a few drops. I remember liking the name, but I had no idea what it was.

Rescue Remedy is the most popular of all the flower essences. People buy it because it rebalances them in times of stress and shock, whether physical or emotional. A million bottles a year sell through British chemists and if you mention the words 'flower remedies' to most people they say, 'Oh yes, Bach' – that's Edward Bach, the British doctor who first developed his range of remedies, including Rescue Remedy, back in the 1930s. But there are hundreds more flower remedies than that.

Fast forward about 15 years and I am reading about a threat posed to the sale of flower remedies by proposed EU legislation which will control and restrict all the available alternative remedies and food supplements in our shops. As a journalist writing about the legislation I find myself in the offices of Living Tree Orchid Essences, makers of essences from their own specially grown orchids but also importers of flower essences from all over the world.

Their headquarters, now in Scotland, revealed a world of remedies. Here are flower essences from Australia, France, Italy, America – north, east, west and south. Here, it seems, are aids to soothe every psychological state and many physical ones, from a broken heart to an anxious or unfocused mind. And yet, if you were to examine the contents of these little bottles chemically, you would find nothing but water and the spirit which preserves it.

To make a flower essence you simply steep the flowers in water or, as they do at Living Tree, just place the flowers over the water. The theory is that the energy or vibration of the flower is caught in the water, or mother tincture, which is then further diluted and bottled to be taken as drops in times of need. Magic or snake oil? Only experience tells and mine is good.

The language used of flower essences and the claims made for them by their makers can be both mystical and miraculous, but in my personal experience they work, and far more specifically and effectively than can be explained away by the placebo effect. It was taking Living Tree's own essence, Clearing the Way, a vibrational essence of the orchid *Phragmipedium Don Wimbur*, that convinced me. A few drops of Clearing the Way had the immediately observable effect of shutting up all those chattering voices in my head that constantly criticized and undermined me. It was like a radio being switched off and the relief was huge. And I wasn't exposing myself to possible dependency or side effects, unlike with prescribed medication. I took the remedy for a few months and then stopped when I felt I no longer needed it. There's a lot of intuition and instinct involved in the use of flower remedies.

Since then I have experimented widely. Some remedies have had no discernible effect. Some I return to again and again. Some have had a remarkable and immediate effect. Perhaps the most dramatic was an Australian Bush Remedy called Sturt Desert Pea. I was looking for something relaxing to take at the end of the day and I actually picked it by mistake. The next day was no fun at all. I felt very depressed and each little setback – a bill in the post, a missed bus – made me tearful. I felt very sad and I cried on and off all day, which is something I very rarely do. But the day after that was sunshine after rain. I woke up, bounced out of bed and found myself singing round the house, all tears gone. Singing is a sure sign that I am happy. The change was dramatic. What was that I'd taken?

Sturt Desert Pea, when I looked it up in Ian White's book *Australian Bush Flower Essences*, claims to deal with accumulated and underlying sadness, clearing it out of the system. In his case histories there were other people who had experienced tears followed by a new cheerfulness. I didn't know that when I took it, which rules out the placebo effect, but it taught me a swift lesson in how specific and effective flower remedies can be.

I never travel now without a small selection of remedies, in the same way that I carry toothpaste and shampoo. I take Five Flower remedy, Dr Bach's original staple. I might take Bush Remedies Emergency Essence on long journeys to even out the exhausting and disorientating effects of travel. And I take whatever essence I am working with at the time, something to focus the mind or boost energy or bring calm.

I have experimented with flower remedies consistently for over a year now, during the course of which my state of mind, my emotional balance and consequently the external details of my life have changed considerably. Flower remedies have helped me to deal with my own moods and, just as important, with the effects of other people's problems. I have given them to friends and relatives and they have also found them to be very helpful, though I am cautious about imposing remedies on others. If a flower remedy isn't the right one it simply has no effect, but when it does hit the spot the effect can be dramatic. When I gave Black Eyed Susan to a hyperactive, stressed-out person, she became very calm and was able to enjoy staying in instead of hurtling about, afraid of missing any fun. Red Suva Lily helped someone else get through the trauma of a break up.

As for me, flower remedies have helped me become a calmer, more open, more trusting and relaxed person. They have made an immediately discernible difference in difficult situations such as going into hospital – Emergency remedy is always useful in stressful situations – and I experience them as a friendly presence in my life, one that is both subtle and powerful. They are one of the most useful tools in my toolbox.

Crystals

When I first began to explore New Age ideas and practices, many years ago, I trod as cautiously as someone making a path across a swamp. For every idea I found valuable there seemed to be 100 that were absolutely batty and could only lead to mind rot and ridicule. I could never shake the voices in my head – my rational, science-trained father, my cynical, brutally questioning colleagues – that would have dismissed my tentative explorations as so much tree-hugging, mantra-chanting, incense-burning nonsense.

So I created boundaries in my head beyond which I would not go, ever. As far outside these boundaries as you could get I placed crystals. People who believed in the magical powers of crystals, people who planted clusters of quartz around their houses or hung them on chains around their necks, people who stuck crystals in front of their computers or swung them on pendulums were away with the fairies. You might as well put your faith in sequinned wings and tinsel crowns. 'If you see me taking an interest in crystals,' I told my friends, 'you'll know I've finally lost it.'

Then one day, years later, I came to a point where I decided that it wasn't rational or reasonable to hold such a blanket prejudice. I decided it was time to put aside a few hours, a day perhaps, to investigate what people claimed for crystals. Experiment would be more scientific than the mental equivalent of garlanding myself with garlic. What tipped me over was my experience with flower remedies. I had found for myself, by direct experience, that something for which there was no currently acceptable scientific explanation actually worked and was valuable, even invaluable. So I might as well go the whole hog, vault over the ring fence of my prejudices and investigate crystals for myself.

I didn't even know at this stage (because I hadn't wanted to look) what exactly it was that crystals were supposed to do or how they were supposed to work. So I did what I suggest you do if you're interested: I went to a crystal shop, a fascinating and beguiling place full of beautiful and extraordinary stones, and I spent not very much money on buying a few crystals which happened to catch my eye. I also bought a couple of books on the subject, one mystical, one quasi-scientific and informative, and I began to read.

The first thing that surprised me very much was that when I followed the advice in the books and simply took a piece of crystal in my hand and meditated with it, relaxing and allowing whatever came into my mind to come, I had a very strong visual experience which changed with each crystal. I tried this contemplation of the crystal with amethyst, fluorite, labradorite, haematite, clear quartz and rose quartz, and each one gave me a series of vivid images that were peculiar to that particular stone and communicated something of its character. I was careful to do this before I read too much in the books so that I would not be influenced by what I read. When I went back to the books, my experience of each stone matched what the collective wisdom about its properties seemed to be.

The next thing I tried, again on the advice of the books, was putting a crystal under my pillow at night. Again, I tried this with different stones. I have done this so often now that I know two things. One is that when you sleep with a crystal under your pillow you sleep very deeply and soundly. The other is that with a crystal under your pillow you can have very vivid and complex dreams whose character can change with the stone. A rose quartz dream is not the same as an amethyst dream. I no longer suffer from insomnia since I started this practice and I lend stones to friends and family who might have trouble sleeping.

Whatever they do and however they work, crystals are beautiful, mysterious and enormously enjoyable objects. They have a powerful allure which can seduce people into a lifelong obsession, whether as a jeweller, a geologist or a crystal healer.

The field of crystal knowledge and lore is huge and it embraces pure science at one end and highly mystical belief at the other. I still think an awful lot of nonsense is talked about crystals, but here's something that works: if you are speeding, stressed, unable to switch off your brain at night, take a piece of haematite, a deep grey metallic stone, very heavy, and place it under your pillow. This makes me sleep.

A New Face, A New You

I don't recommend major retail therapy because it's no more than expensive Elastoplast. Everyone knows you shouldn't shop for food when you're hungry and it's better not to shop for clothes when you're miserable. But lipstick – that's different. For not much money you get something bright, pretty, sweet-smelling, ego-boosting – a treat. And it doesn't make you fat.

There is nothing at all frivolous or trivial about this. The more dire the circumstances a woman finds herself in, the more power cosmetics and grooming have to hold her together. During the Balkan wars the women of Sarajevo did their best to look fabulous under siege. Each time they flew in, women war correspondents loaded their luggage with lipsticks and shampoos to give to the Bosnian women. Looking good is a punchy, immediate way to show the bastards they can't get you down. It's a beautiful way to rebel.

There are ways for men to do this too. Putting on a happy face is the theme of the opening scene of one of my favourite movies, the Bob Fosse biopic *All That Jazz*. A hungover Fosse, played by Roy Scheider, hits the bathroom, turns up the bouncy baroque music, pops the pills, splashes in the eyedrops and faces his mirror with an adrenalin-boosting 'It's showtime!' Life is showtime. Sometimes you have to make up to fake it. It's a cheap trick, but it's fun and it works.

Tribal Mothering

Here's the dilemma. You live in a small community. Everybody knows your name. There can be a comfort in this, but no anonymity, no freedom, which is one reason why the world's cities are crowded with people who have come from villages.

So here's another dilemma. You live in a large city, a community which often doesn't feel like a community at all. Nobody knows your name. There is freedom in this, but no support. Where, in all the millions of people around you, are the village elders? The wise women? The young braves to come to your rescue? The tribal mothers?

I never felt this lack of tribal support as acutely as when I was bringing up young teenagers as a single parent in the city. I saw how easy and dangerous it would be for my children's heartbeats to tune themselves to urban jungle drums rather than the quieter pulse of their own home. I knew that I needed reinforcement from a bigger group. My own family is typically scattered, separated by long journeys. We manage to gather for Christmases and birthdays, but there's none of that frequent casual contact that makes extended families out of nuclear ones and keeps us all bonded into the pattern of each other's daily lives. And strangers aren't what they were. Nobody wants to get involved. People are afraid of being abused if they check a teenager, of being misunderstood if they comfort a crying child. The result is isolation. Parents in a society like this have a hard job holding boundaries all alone.

One day we had a big family crisis, one that happens to other people and you hope never happens to you. I'd been away for the weekend, leaving my 15-year-old daughter staying with the family of a friend. When I returned to my home all my instincts told me something was wrong. Maybe it was the slightly rearranged furniture. Maybe it was the lights burning everywhere. Maybe it was the muddy footprints over the sofa. Definitely it was the fact that my daughter was somehow at home after all and making the unprecedented claim that she'd been cleaning the house.

Party time. Thanks to neighbours, the truth came out fast. My elder daughter, with the help of a lot of deceit, had returned home with her friends and invited 120 people, most of them strangers, into my now battered and grubby house. Within minutes I realized that all her close friends, the little toads, had also lied to their parents about where they'd been and had joined in the vandalism of my home. As soon as my delinquent daughter realized I was serious about phoning each family up in turn, she sheepishly handed over her phone book.

It was tribal mothering time. One by one I asked each of those parents to turn up at my house the next day, with their daughters, and thrash the whole thing out. One by one they arrived, embarrassed daughter in tow, and we sat in a big talking circle and began to say what we felt about what had happened. I talked. The mothers talked. The daughters got their chance to talk. We decided on appropriate punishments. We cleared the air. We ended up with reminiscences and laughter. We made friends. We knew that, in the maelstrom of parenting teenagers, we weren't alone. It was tribal mothering and it was a huge help and comfort over the next few years. The parents knew they had support at the end of a phone line. The girls knew that there were rules. It wasn't a matter of deceiving one parent any more. They knew we would communicate. And, 10 years later, those girls are still good friends, now impressive, hard-working adults with their delinquent years behind them.

You don't have to be a single parent to find the concept of the tribe a huge comfort. A group that is going through the same life experiences as you are can be a life-saver. At different times in my life I've found myself part of different groups – colleagues, students, choristers, artists – that have led to lifelong friendships. Group energy can carry forward a person who would be flagging on their own. It is different from normal friendship because it has a framework, a purpose. The thing is, whatever you are going through, you don't have to do it alone.

And you don't have to wait for somebody to find you. You can be the one who stands up, as I did on that night, and says, 'Is there anyone else out there who is in the same situation?' A successful tribe looks after its own and the good news is you don't have to be born into one. You can always make your own.

Talk to a Tree

There was a song that used to make me laugh when I was little. 'I talk to the trees – that's why they put me away…' So I don't talk to trees, but sometimes I let trees talk to me. No, of course they don't talk to me either. What I mean is, sometimes I feel a lot better when I've spent time near a tree and we've just been quiet together.

It's always worth listening to a tree. They have a sound world of their own and the more attentively you can sit with them and open your ears and mind, the more tuned in you will become to the life, the stillness, the strength, the slow growth, the power of sanctuary which a tree offers.

The best moments of a stay in Crete were spent in the shade, leaning against the trunk of an ancient olive tree at the foot of the Samaria Gorge. I had simply sat there to rest and pay attention to the life of the gorge – the million-year-old flow of the rocks, the scent of the fig trees, the featherlight dance of insects swimming in the air currents, the constant tread of thousands of walkers in the dusty path, up and down. Then that tree got to me. After I'd spent half an hour in its company I felt as if I had been time-travelling. I had detached myself from the flickering existence of the insects, even the walkers with their soft, tired flesh and brittle bones, and I had tuned into a planetary rhythm, the infinitely slow ebb and flow that was recorded on the rock walls and in the thick twisted sinews of the olive trees. Time out of time is what it takes to rebalance as a human being, and time out of time is what great trees offer. It's what makes trees into teachers.

I remembered, as I got up, that people can have good ideas under the influence of trees. Hippocrates of Kos healed people under a plane tree. Isaac Newton understood the nature of gravity under an apple tree. The Buddha found enlightenment under the bodhi tree. I'm not saying that you'll discover the secrets of the universe or attain enlightenment in the company of trees, but if you want to gain perspective, release cares, unravel a problem or simply retune your heartstrings, a tree is the place to go.

Use a Life Coach

Three times in my life I've used a life coach and each time they've given me the encouragement and the fresh thinking to make major positive changes in my life that I wouldn't have made without their help.

The first time I felt I needed outside help was when I seemed to have everything a girl could possibly want. I had a weekly column in a national newspaper and a well-paid executive job as women's editor, complete with expenses and nice new company car. I had a husband, two adorable little children and a pretty house with a lovely garden in the suburbs. And somehow, with all this on my plate, I felt as if I were draining away.

I can't remember who or what sent me to a life-coaching firm, but I found myself sitting sceptically in front of Ben, who was all of 25 years old, thinking, *How can you possibly help me to make a difference to my life*? Eight weeks later, with the help of Ben's intensive twice-weekly sessions, I had offloaded 80 percent of my work and hung on to the same income. I'd handed over my executive role and was happily being paid for staying at home with my children and just writing my column. As each day at home passed I felt veils of stress lift and float away. I still use the goal-setting skills I learned from Ben, who is now a very high flyer himself in a merchant bank.

About 10 years later I found myself in a different situation. I had been a columnist on another national newspaper for 10 years, as well as a freelance writer for other papers and magazines, and was still with the children, but minus the husband. My relationship with the paper was coming to an end, but I'd been a columnist for so long that I could only think that I had to do the same song-and-dance act somewhere else. I was sitting in front of editors and swearing that I would love to write for them, and it wasn't true.

So this time I went to see Jo Ellen. Jo Ellen was a coach who worked with a lot of creative clients and had a background in music and the theatre. I thought she might have a different take and I expectantly waited for her to start the same sort of 'to do' lists I'd done with Ben. Instead she listened to me carefully, asked some pertinent questions and then said, 'I hear you say you've done this and achieved that and sorted the other. Have you ever stopped?'

I was shocked, and my eyes filled with tears. Were you allowed to stop? Was stopping an option? As the idea sunk in and I began to think if and how I could afford to take a break, I began to feel liberated, as though someone had given me the keys to my own prison. I mentally ran through my savings and decided I could afford to take the heat off myself for three months. By the time I walked back through my own front door I'd decided, as an experiment, that for three months I was only going to do work that positively excited me. And I was going to take a day a week and go to art school.

Within those three months I'd signed on for a two-year part-time art foundation course, while still working as a freelance journalist. I figured that if the art course proved too much, I could drop out. But I completed it and was offered a job as art critic on a daily paper. That was the most enjoyable and enriching job I ever had. Two years later I graduated with an MA in design and illustration, while still earning my living as a freelance journalist, because I'd discovered that when you're powered by enthusiasm and you're really focused on what you want, things fall into place. I actually earned more money in my years as a part-time art student than I had before. Of course I was working twice as hard, but then I loved it.

I only went to see Jo Ellen once because she gave me one big idea and that made all the difference.

I went to Fiona two years after I finished my MA because I'd slightly run out of steam again. The thing is, the circumstances of one's life are constantly changing, and Fiona, who was a constant source of encouragement and positive thinking, led me to the realization of a long-held fantasy.

I live and work in the city and I've always fantasized about owning a place in the country. Fiona works by blasting you with ideas and in one brain-storming session she made me see that there were loads of ways I could get a foothold in the country which didn't involve buying and selling or making that scary commitment to pulling up roots.

I started looking at places to let and by the end of the year I had started paying rent on a furnished flat in a village with a heart-stopping view over woods, valleys and fields. Now I can go there and hear owls, watch buzzards, gaze at the full moon shining on the autumn mist or the constantly changing light as summer clouds drift by. I've learned a lot, and one thing, one big thing, I've learned is that I don't want to live in the country full time. I've learned to love my dirty, overcrowded, multi-cultural city much more. It was worth going to Fiona to be kick-started into doing something about a dream, even if – maybe especially if – that dream turned out to be different from the way I'd been dreaming it.

Anyone can call themselves a life coach, so beware. Go on personal recommendation. Compare costs – a life coach can be expensive, but if they help you make the life you want, it's worth it. Find out as much about them as you can. If you don't like them, don't go. If they're any good at their job, they should help you make a real difference to your life.

How to Be a River Goddess

I had only set off for a walk. I was going to walk along the wooded ridge on the west side of Richmond Park, descend to cross Ham Common and walk through Ham village to the banks of the River Thames. Then I would turn right and follow the towpath to Petersham, cut up River Lane and climb to the top of Richmond Hill where I'd left my car. It should have been a good walk, but it turned into a great walk.

When I finally reached the riverbank at Ham I found that I had left something very important out of my calculations: I had forgotten to check the state of the tide. The Thames at Richmond is a tidal river and at high tide the towpath often floods. So as I turned to walk towards Petersham, I found that the path was covered with a couple of inches of water and that the water was rising. My way home was flooding.

I had a choice. I could turn back the way I had come, which would be long and dreary because it was nearing sunset, the park would close and I would have to follow the road. *Or*, I thought, as I looked down at the dark brown water which was lapping at the toes of my shoes, *I could paddle*.

I looked ahead. I didn't have far to go. There was only half a mile of flooded towpath between me and Petersham, where I could turn off into the woods. The rising tide hid the edge of the riverbank, but I had walked this path often and I knew where the river lay, so there was no danger of falling in. What was the worst that could happen? I would get my feet wet and, possibly, tread on something unpleasant that lay below the water. Long boring walk back the way I'd come? Paddle? I bent down and took off my shoes. I was wearing tights, but they were just going to get wet. I turned up my trousers and stepped into the flood tide.

At that point I lost touch with ordinary reality and entered a new world. At first the water was just above my ankles. I could feel the stony surface of the path beneath the soles of my feet. The incoming water laid a hush over everything. There was nobody else about. Gradually, the water crept up to my knees. I had to stop and roll my trousers up again. Voices floated over the river from the far bank. Suddenly I stumbled. The path had dropped away below my feet and the cold water was suddenly up above my knees.

I stood and worked out what had happened. I had reached a point where a side gulley left the main towpath and was carrying the flood water in a little torrent into a field which lay below the level of the river bank. I realized, as

I watched the tide water gushing down this channel into the field, that I hadn't thought about changes in level, cross-paths or cross-currents.

My trousers were really wet now, no point in rolling them up further, but my coat was going to get wet, so I took that off and tied it round my shoulders. There was nobody about at all. I stood in a wide sheet of fast-flowing water. If I slipped and fell or got out of my depth and was swept into the river nobody would know. But I was halfway to my exit by now, the little wood which I knew I could climb into. I was going to get wetter, but I didn't see how I could drown. Feeling with my bare feet, I advanced very carefully, crossing the dip in the towpath, and found myself back on higher ground, though I was still in the fast-flowing river up to my thighs.

Then the path dropped beneath my feet again and this time I went in above my waist. At this point of no return I was swept with exhilaration. The sun was setting behind me and a red cloud-streaked sky was reflected in the river's shining wide surface. As the trees around me grew dark, the river grew light. A little fleet of ducks sailed past me. A shimmering hush prevailed. All I could hear were river sounds: the surge and splash of my own body forging through the water, the thin sound human voices make as they cross water, the wind in the branches and the running of the water through the drowned grasses.

As I ploughed and splashed nearer the little wood, I could hear a man and a woman talking. I climbed out of the water and over a bank into the trees, dripping and running with river water, my dry shoes in my hand. In front of me, in the twilit dusk of the wood, stood a startled young couple, dumbfounded at the sight of me, a figure appearing miraculously and silently from the depths of the river. When he found his voice the young man said, 'What are you? A river goddess or something?'

I was wet through, cold, muddy and bedraggled, but I felt like a river goddess alright. I had left my normal element, dry land, for an element which was much more mysterious and unpredictable. There had been a point, waist deep in the sunset river, when I had felt a part of the flooding, twilit world around me. I'd faced a little danger, but I'd survived. I'd taken a physical risk, but it had paid off. I'd got soaked, but I felt positively giggly. I'd thrown being cautious and sensible out of the window and been natural instead, and it felt glorious. I'd stepped out of my regulated city world and gone primitive. If that's what it feels like to be a river goddess, then, yes, for half an hour I was one.

The famous psychoanalyst Carl Jung once said that if every man and woman could experience being primitive for five minutes a day then he would have no patients.

Maybe this exhilaration, this adrenalin rush, this heightened sense of being a physical creature is behind the rising passion for extreme sports. I don't want to throw myself off a mountain, but I know that the following things are also an antidote to computer-bound, television-enslaved, car-incarcerated 21st-century life: going barefoot and feeling the world beneath the soles of your feet, walking, running, cartwheeling on the beach, climbing hills, swimming in a river, a lake or best of all the sea, climbing trees and rocks, swinging or turning upside down, dancing, paddling, surfing, jumping waves, wearing as few clothes as possible, allowing yourself to get wet in the rain.

Do any of these things sound familiar? We did them all as children and we felt fantastic. To feel as exhilarated and as connected to life as you did when you were a child, all you have to do is take off your shoes and skip out of your element.

When the Sea is your Dinner Date

I thank my friend Susie for a trick that transforms the experience of being alone. Susie and her mother and I were on holiday and our evening ritual was a stroll along the waterfront past all the little *tavernas* with their display cases of fresh fish and delicious vegetable dishes while we decided which one we wanted to eat in that night.

Every single *taverna* had inviting little tables set on the water's edge looking out over the bay with a backdrop of sheer mountains sloping down into the clear green water. No matter which *taverna* we chose, we would take the table and turn it square on to the view so that all three of us could sit and look out to sea as the sun went down. 'And this,' said Susie exuberantly, waving her hand over the sea, the mountains, the sunset and rocks, 'is your dinner date for tonight.'

Susie and her mother had to go back to work after a week but I decided to stay on by myself. I loved the place and I like being by myself, but anyone who travels alone knows that dinner can be the most difficult time. It's easy being on your own during the day, but eating alone in the evening feels much more solitary, especially when most of the other tables are crowded with holidaying families and couples.

But I had the sea as my dinner date. I had nobody to distract me from concentrating on the imperceptibly shifting colours of rock and sky and water. I had nobody blocking my view of the last fishing boats coming in, the lights coming on over the water, the fading of the mountains through soft shades of blue and lilac as the sun went down. Instead of struggling to make conversation like some of the couples round me, or dealing with tired, fractious children like some of the families, I could focus on the last red mountain tops. I could lift my glass of wine to the primal miracle of the moon rising above the rim of the sea. I took just as much care choosing my solitary viewpoint each night as I had when I was one of three. Because the sea was my dinner date I was never bored. Because the sea was my dinner date I never felt deprived. I felt full.

But you can't take the sea everywhere with you. And sometimes we all have to be alone. And it can be hard. I know a seasoned single traveller who lost weight in Athens because she couldn't pluck up the courage to go into restaurants alone. Sometimes people who run restaurants are mean to single eaters and make them feel even smaller than they do already. Sometimes they are charming and lovely and make you feel wonderful. But not knowing which experience you are going to get adds to the fear many people have of being alone.

Some people already think that other diners will think they are sad and unlovable. They should take a tip from a woman I know who assumes that if she's alone, everyone will think she's mysterious and glamorous.

But what does it matter what other people might think when your companion is the whole world? It doesn't have to be the sea. It can be a busy city pavement, a crowded restaurant, a place where you can watch other people rather than a view. Or, if you are alone at home, hooray – you are spoilt for choice. Your dinner date needn't be the television, though that is many people's companion of choice. It can be Tolstoy, Rembrandt, a copy of *Vogue*, a book of verse, a vase of flowers. Alone is never alone once you turn your attention out to the world.

Forever Creating

It can be paralysing trying to create something good. Instead of seeing what we do as a fluid process that can be changed, we are intimidated by the concept of perfection and comparison. Children who create freely when they are little stop in their tracks when they come up against the idea of perfection. Their flower doesn't look like a real flower, so they stop drawing flowers forever. If we are not to be permanently blocked and perpetually self-critical, we have to look at creativity differently.

I heard a programme on the radio about a village in Africa where the women continually decorate their houses with intricate patterns of coloured mud. They are famous for their beautiful houses and their innate artistry and they accept their work as a transitory thing. The sun cracks the mud and the rain washes it away, and the next season they re-create their decorated houses knowing that, however glorious their work, it won't last forever.

The villages attract visitors, photographers and tourists. And the tourists marvel at the houses and are shocked that so much work is so impermanent. 'Isn't there a way,' they ask, 'that the women can fix their work in cement or translate their skills into artefacts that tourists can buy and hang on their walls and keep forever?'

The village women think the tourists are very funny. 'They have their little forevers,' says one, 'but we are forever creating.'

When you look at creativity as a process instead of a means to produce perfection, it frees you up enormously. My friend Gloria Karpinski keeps a note above her desk to free her when she gets stuck writing a book. 'Process not product,' it says. 'Privilege not pressure.' The process is the point. Even great works of art are often just stills from the movie of the artist's mind. They don't leap up fully formed from nowhere, they are landmarks on a long journey, and the journey is as important as the destination.

To produce we must be able to make endless mistakes and often the mistakes themselves are starting-points for fresh approaches and new ideas. When I sit paralysed at my desk or drawing board, thinking I should be producing something great, I have to remind myself that it really doesn't matter where you start, the point is to prime the pump, to make for the sake of making without worrying about the finished product. That will come. Unless we are forever creating, there won't be any forevers at all.

The Uses of Silence

The cure for noise is silence. Sometimes music feels like the cure for everything – the upbeat music that sets your heart and body dancing, the solemn music that allows you to cry, the haunting music that lets you dream. But there are times to turn off the music, because silence is what you need to breathe, to uncoil, to return to a state of balance and hear the quiet call of your own heart. When life is hectic I sometimes close a door and enter a room where there is no sound but my own breathing and I feel a profound relief.

It is very hard to find silence in a world where mechanical noise is everywhere. You can't shop, have your hair cut, check into a hotel, exercise at a gym, even fill your car with petrol without the accompaniment of someone else's soundtrack. They have even put music into bookshops, the last refuge of the peaceful browser, and a train company has just decided to put constant television into train carriages, even though everyone I know treats a train ride as an opportunity for reading and contemplation.

But if you seek it out, there is more silence in the world than noise. You can find it if you go deep into the interior of people and buildings and you can find it on the planet's surface. Recently I stood on a friend's doorstep at midnight and felt myself expand into the silence of the night. It was deep in the hill country of the north of England and there were no cars, no radios, no mobile phones. All I could see was the single light of a distant farm and all I could hear was a nearby waterfall and the wind in the trees. I could feel myself become calmer, taller.

Silence lets you grow. In fact I'd say that you can't grow without it. I think that unwanted sounds are like a physical assault. Something in us shrinks at the constant battering of noise and it's only when we find a source of silence and become conscious of it and receive it that we realize how exhausting is the onslaught of the sounds we haven't chosen.

You can find silence in an empty room. There is silence in an empty church or temple. There is silence in art, in the depths of a great painting. There is silence in a vase of flowers or in the sky. And the place where there is always silence is in our own depths.

Choose a quiet place. Close your eyes to the world. Sit comfortably. Breathe gently and tune in to that inner silence and you have found a constant source of renewal.

Darkness

True darkness is a refuge and a revelation. I remember standing in a church one Christmas Eve at a candlelit service, at the moment of darkness when every light was out, and suddenly having a sense of the real power of the Christmas image of a light shining in darkness

Once, not so long ago, the whole world was dark. Then there was electricity and now we have become cut off from the stars. We are a neon, halogen, flood, laser, lightbulb dazzled generation and most of us have never experienced true darkness at all. What we think of as darkness is no more than a deeper kind of shade. But thousands of generations before us lived with true night-time darkness, a depth of darkness in which the light of a candle was a wonder, an image of huge power.

We use the word *darkness* as a synonym for the bad, but it isn't. Darkness is good. Darkness is the soil out of which we grow and to which we return. It is dark in the womb when we grow slowly, cell by cell. We seek darkness at night when we need to shut down our physical and mental body for rest and repair. It is dark in the earth where bulbs and seeds begin to unfold before spring. It is dark in the places where we dream – cinemas and theatres and our own beds. Sometimes those dreams are nightmares, but the darkness is what we need to unravel all our thoughts, both good and bad. Without darkness, as prisoners and victims of torture in their cruelly lighted cells can testify, there is no rest, only madness.

It makes me sad that children are growing into adulthood in cities all over the world without truly experiencing darkness and its revelation, a glimpse of the astonishing, mysterious universe of which our planet is a tiny part. Some people feel fear and nothingness when they gaze at the night sky and realize how infinitesimally small they are, but I find it comforting. It gives me an epic scale against which to measure my little preoccupations, my mayfly life.

In the city, among the lights, I am sometimes astonished by the sight of the moon over the rooftops. It is easy to forget. In the country I hang out of my window at night, transfixed by the brilliant golden glow of Mars in the east, by the creamy dust of the Milky Way. I live in a cloudy country where a clear night sky isn't guaranteed, even if you can escape from light pollution, so I try to travel each year to somewhere where there is true darkness and I can see a dazzling night sky – a Mediterranean island, a North African desert. I will never forget the magic of sailing on an Ethiopian lake at midnight where the brightest stars were so bright they made tracks on the water. It's the most beautiful of paradoxes that we need to experience deep darkness in order to see the most brilliant of lights.

Life is a Work in Progress

I can't bear it when people say they're a failure. Few things upset me more than seeing someone, especially somebody young, crumpled in a miserable heap because they think they're a failure. If that's you, stop it. Peel the label off and throw it away. Right now. Because you're not a failure, you're a work in progress. You've just hit a bit where you're not progressing.

Maybe I was just born this way, but even on the most stomach-turning downs on the roller-coaster of life it never occurs to me to think of myself as a failure. So something didn't work out. Maybe it was a big thing like a job or a marriage and I'm broken-hearted, but that still doesn't make me a failure. It makes me a person whose marriage broke up or who's reached a place which may require some creative CV writing. The word *failure* is like a black line drawn under a column, but there are no black lines in life. Everything is fluid. Everything changes. Even the darkest moments are temporary stages in a long unfolding journey which only really ends in death. And maybe not then.

Even as a child I worked out that life was full of surprises and you could never know the sum of it till it was over – and even then it was open to interpretation, otherwise why would people keep rewriting biographies and history? I was really pleased to find out that someone, Solon the Athenian lawgiver in fact, had got into the book of quotations back in the fifth century BC when he said, 'Call no man happy till he is dead.' Call no man or woman a failure either.

If I reject the idea of failure, it's because of its finality. Somebody who thinks of themselves as a failure is accepting a self-imposed defeat and it paralyses them. But life is movement and the important thing is to keep moving, try another angle, have another go. That way you learn there's the world of difference between reaching a dead end and setting up home in it. Above all, never, ever send out change of address cards.

Be your Own Resource

We all know more than we think we do. We've all done things that worked, things that excited us, that gave us glimpses of ourselves as we'd like to be, life as we'd like to experience it. And then we've forgotten.

This is a great mystery. Why is it so easy to forget even the good things, the moments of understanding and insight, the moments when the whole pattern becomes clear? I think it's because life is so fast-moving, so fragmented and so complex. It's not just our own story that we are living, it's the related stories of millions of other people, all with their own confusions.

The air is full of static. Newspapers, television, radio, the internet, mobile phones, texts and e-mails, books, the cinema, music, art, theatre, fashion, shopping, advertising, politics, bureaucracy, other people's demands on us at work, families – all this is clamouring for our attention before we've even spent five minutes paying attention to one person who is important to us. There is no time to think, no space to feel.

If you live life unconsciously, allowing your time and movements to be driven by external forces, then you are in danger of leaving the ground altogether, of becoming a piece of tumbleweed blowing across a desert floor. The look I see on many people's faces, especially travelling to work in my city, is one of exhausted bewilderment. *How did I get here? How do I get out?* It doesn't matter how old you are. If anything, it is the younger people, people in their twenties, thirties, forties, who sigh that they're shattered.

If this is you, nobody is going to stop the roundabout but you. It's not about changing your life all in one go. It's about finding a moment of authenticity, a moment of self-truth. These moments are the places you can stand on to change the world. As a starting-point you need to make your own version of everything you've ever done that worked – for you.

Your starting place is a moment of quietness (though you can do this with friends) and something to write with. Once the momentum is going this is a wholly pleasurable, even inspiring exercise. I remember doing it with Ben, my first coach, and he always said it was his favourite part of the job.

Think back to those moments when you felt fully yourself, fully alive. Were you five years old? Fifteen? Thirty? Where were you? What were you doing? Who were you with? Was it something you did once or something that is integrated into your life? Was it a moment of play or part of your working life?

Would you love to do it again? How did you feel afterwards? Was there a hangover of some kind or were you inspired, energized?

And there's another kind of list, a list of the times when you were in doubt or difficulty and survived. What got you out of it? Was it help from friends, taking control yourself, learning new skills, changing your life, having medical help, following a spiritual practice, taking a stand, going on a workshop, reading a book, going to law, seeing a therapist, building on a chance encounter with a stranger or simply taking time out – a sabbatical, a holiday or a gap year? Did you take notes, keep a diary? Dig them out.

I don't know what any of these answers will be for you. But when you've gathered all this material (and it may take some time), you will. And you will have your resource book. Put it together. Stick a label on it. Present it to yourself as formally and as attractively as you like. 'Everything I've Ever Done That Worked. By me.'

The Refugee's Guide to Being Human

Sometimes people lose everything. The crisis that comes into their lives isn't one of the heart, the ego or the bank balance. They haven't lost a job, a lover or even a limb. Their view of their future hasn't simply vanished as a castle in the air quivers and melts in the mind, it has crumbled into real dust before their physical eyes. A familiar wall hides a sniper. A beloved home explodes in flames. The men who support you are killed or have vanished. The women you love and honour are raped. The children starve. The country lies in ruins. What, in these extremes of human experience, works?

One hot May day in 1999 I walked on a Macedonian hillside among people who were at the edge of living what a human life involves. The hillside had been bulldozed bare of all vegetation, even grass. The green hills of the Balkans were all around, but here wire fences marked out blinding acres of rough stones. I was in Cigrane, the latest refugee camp created in Macedonia for the thousands of refugees fleeing across the borders from Kosovo. It was for Albanian Kosovans who had abandoned their homes to Serbian militia and who had spent days and weeks trekking through the mountains to a place of safety.

Cigrane wasn't a place where anyone wanted to be. It was so new and raw that tents were still being erected and families were sleeping out on uncushioned stones on the bare mountainside. Outside the camp gates waited red buses crammed with exhausted people who had queued to walk across the Macedonian border. I had seen the buses earlier waiting at the border post and the shocked, drained and exhausted faces of the people in them were like no human faces I had ever seen before. They were the faces of people who had surrendered, the unfocused, burnt-out faces of people at the edge of endurance. When I saw them I thought I knew what the Jews looked like on the trains that took them to the concentration camps.

Five thousand people a day were coming into Cigrane. While the newest group of refugees waited passively in the buses, inside the gates I walked about and talked to the people who had already been there a night. A system was beginning to establish itself. Where tents had been erected and blankets distributed, the human urge to create a home was asserting itself.

People had no more than the clothes they had been wearing when they fled the Serbs. To have clean clothes they had to lie naked under their blankets while their clothes dried on the guy ropes of their tent. Mothers with babies queued in the hot May sun for the daily ration of three disposable nappies a day. Further down the hillside a lorry unloaded the sole food allowance of one roll of bread a day. There was another queue at a trestle table set up by the Red Cross to register people looking for lost relatives.

Everywhere I walked I could feel a palpable atmosphere of bewilderment, fatigue and frustration. These were the surface emotions stirred up by the chaos of the camp. Beneath the minute by minute anxiety of trying to function in this raw, hostile environment each individual was holding deeper feelings of loss, grief and a terrible fear for the future.

And yet in the most difficult circumstances the human spirit irresistibly asserts itself. Children were playing and laughing by the water pipes. Little twig brooms already stood outside the doors of the tents as a witness to the effort to create order out of overwhelming disorder.

I will never forget standing on the most exposed area of the camp, a white slope of sharp stones scattered with the belongings of the small family groups of people who had spent the night on the open mountainside. I was talking to a weary middle-aged couple about their sleepless night when a striking little group came straggling up the hillside towards us. Like Mother Courage, Begishe, a 32-year-old woman, grubby but spirited, was leading her raggle-taggle band of five children up the hill. They were dusty-faced, weary, their arms full of bags and blankets and babies. They had been sleeping under the stars and on the stones of Cigrane for five days. Before that Begishe had led them through the mountains from village to village, ever since the Serbian militia had attacked their village and driven them up into makeshift shelters in the forest. Their father was in Germany, but the dusty little family radiated a tough spirit of survival and resilience.

As they stood talking to the older couple I expressed my inadequate sympathy for their situation and it was my awkward words of kindness rather than their hardship which brought tears to their eyes. I wanted to know what it was that gave them the spirit and courage to keep going in these extreme and chaotic circumstances. It was the older woman who told me.

'We do everything together,' she said simply. 'We give each other moral support. We are very human to each other.'

It was a very striking and humbling lesson. When everything intangible has gone – status, worldly identity, optimism for the future, ambition – people can still be human to each other. When everything tangible has gone – home, land, family, farm animals, clothes and possessions – people can still be human to each other. Being human is all they have left.

What did this woman mean, homeless on her open mountainside, by being human? After all, the gunmen who had driven these people out of their homes and country were being human too. I've thought often about this and I think that being human means being vulnerable and open. It means being in sympathy with other people and knowing that you are not different from them. It means being part of one organism, not safe and not separate. It means abandoning roles, expectations, judgements and opposition. It means losing the need to control other people. It means being responsive to your environment and not shut off from it, let alone seized by the need to exploit and destroy it. It means reaching out rather than shutting off. It certainly *doesn't* mean discriminating, oppressing, excluding and even killing.

Good fortune and bad fortune can both encourage a sense of humanity. Good fortune does it by making us relaxed, trusting and unafraid, bad fortune by making us recognize our irreducible human nature and our interdependency with others. But good fortune carries the danger of complacency and detachment from other people's experience. The enclaves of the rich aren't famous for their humanity, however many cheques the rich may sign for the poor. It is ironic that the great qualities of openness, generosity and kindness often only surface in extreme circumstances – the London Blitz, September 11th. In circumstances of overwhelming threat, when everything familiar has gone, being human is all that works.

Like everything else in this book, when the circumstances change, the lesson is in danger of being lost. I once heard Ram Dass speak and he said that the challenge of life is to keep your heart open in hell. They were striking words, but when I remember those Kosovans in the stones and dust, I wonder if it isn't easier to keep your heart open in hell when your heart is all that is left. The challenge is to stay human when the complexity of daily life returns, along with the suffocation of possessions, the seeking and maintaining of status. That is one reason why I wrote this book. Time and again, in difficult circumstances, I have found something that worked, only to forget it again when the difficulty passed. I know one truth: as sure as the sun rises, life will get difficult again. Which is why I hope that by writing these things down I will remember them for myself and why I pass them on to you, in the sincere hope that they will help in the magnificent but sometimes overwhelming business of being human.

Reading and Resource List

Books are an ever-present source of inspiration. This is a short list of books and other resources that I have found helpful and friendly. If I were to list the books that have inspired, stimulated, comforted and enriched me over the course of a lifetime, it would take another whole book.

Self-help books and handbooks perform a very useful function, but the more challenging the books and the more deeply you read, the more you will get out of your life. Explore it all – poetry, philosophy, fiction, science, biography, travel and memoir.

To get an idea of how a person's life can be inspired and influenced by their reading, I suggest you look at *An Autobiography* by M. K. Gandhi (1929; Penguin, 1982) or *The Golden String* by Bede Griffith (Fount, 1979).

Performance: Revealing the Orpheus Within by Anthony Rooley (Element Books, 1984). A musician's look at the relationship between preparation and inspiration.

The Meditator's Handbook by David Fontana (HarperCollins, 1992).

A clear and comprehensive account of different forms of meditation with plenty of practical exercises.

The Miracle of Mindfulness by Thich Nhat Hanh (Rider, 1991). A small classic of Buddhist meditation, written so clearly a child could understand.

A Woman in Your Own Right by Anne Dickson (Quartet, 1982). The standard work on assertiveness training.

Emotional Freedom Technique – there are few books but many websites. Tap 'emotional freedom technique' into Google and you will find plenty of leads.

www.meridiantherapies.org has an instant two-minute stress relief technique you can follow on the screen.

Spiritual Fitness by Caroline Reynolds (HarperCollins, 2001). A specific course of exercises you can follow to deepen your experience of life. *Sabbath Rest* by Wayne Muller (Lion, 2000). A heartfelt and well-argued case for restoring rest and rhythm into stressed-out modern lives.

The Mozart Effect by Don Campbell (Hodder & Stoughton, 2002). A well-argued and densely illustrated case for the crucial role of music in our life and health.

A Compendium of Flower Essences by Clare G. Harvey, Peter Tadd and Don Dennis, published by International Flower Essence Repertoire at Achamore House, Isle of Gigha, Argyll, Scotland PA4 1AD; Tel: 01583 505385. They are very knowledgeable and also run residential courses on the Isle of Gigha. Their website is www.healingflowers.com. The Australian Bush Essences are also widely available from branches of Neal's Yard and Fresh and Wild. Their website is www.ausflowers.com.au.

I also recommend the following books by Ian White:

– *Australian Bush Flower Essences* (Findhorn Press, 1993).

– *Australian Bush Flower Healing* (Bantam, 1999).

The definitive layman's guide to cognitive behaviour therapy is *Feeling Good* by David D. Burns, MD (Avon Health, 1999). Also recommended is *The Feeling Good Handbook* by David D. Burns, MD (Plume, 2000).

Be Your Own Life Coach by Fiona Harrold (Hodder Mobius, 2001). A brisk and practical introduction to life coaching from one of the UK's most high-profile and experienced coaches.

Crystal Power, Crystal Healing by Michael Gienger (Cassell and Co, 1998). There are plenty of books about crystals and many of them, frankly, are more poetry and fairytale than science, but this has very good photographs and some actual geological information along with the healing associations of each stone.

The Artist's Way by Julia Cameron (Tarcher/Putnam, 1998). This is a classic of self-help and creativity for anyone and everyone who doubts their ability to be creative. It is well written, practical, very encouraging and the focus for a number of support groups.

Finding your Own North Star by Martha Beck (Piatkus, 2001). This is where I found the Beauty Way, but Martha Beck has plenty of good techniques to help you shut out the noise and find your own way.

Where Two Worlds Touch and *Barefoot on Holy Ground*, both by Gloria Karpinski (Ballantine, 1990 and 2001). Gloria sees life as a spiritual journey and brings a lifetime of practice to her understanding of how we can stay in touch with the spirit in the midst of busy lives.

Molecules of Emotion by Candace B. Pert (Prentice Hall, 1997). This is the science bit. Psychoneuroimmunologist Candace Pert explains, in terms that I can understand, how emotions are chemistry and vice versa. She also gives practical suggestions for helping our body to be its own healer and tranquillizer.

Everything I've Ever Learned About Love

Continuing on from *Everything I've Ever Done That Worked*, this new work is a love letter to life in the form of a book about love.

In this collection of memories, insights, anecdotes and observations Lesley will map her lifelong personal relationship with love. As daughter, grand-daughter, relative, friend, pupil, lover, confidante, traveller, writer, artist, wife and mother she has danced with love in all its guises. She has been nurtured, abandoned, seduced, enchanted, enraptured, valued, floored and wounded, distracted, obsessed, desired, hurt and redeemed by love.

As a writer and observer and as the witness to other people's experience, she has thought about and reflected on love as well as being its object and subject. Not a day of her life has gone by in which love has not been a presence, whether in fulfilment and enjoyment or absence and longing.

Whoever reads this book will be re-educated in love. They will understand better the impulses that drive their own emotions and relationships and how to resist self destruction and harm. They will learn to appreciate the moods and weathers of love from altruism and compassion through affection and loyalty to desire, passion and obsession.

And they will understand one important truth, that, counter to a culture which focuses on sexual gratification and the single relationship with one other human being, the Right One, love, is to be found everywhere. The love of one's life may be another human being but that is only one aspect of the great multi-faceted love affair open to everyone – the love of life itself.

Both Lesley and Hay House Publishers hope you enjoy this extracted essay from *Everything I've Ever Learned About Love.*

Available from all good bookshops or by calling Hay House Publishers on 020 8962 1230.

Set Your Compass to Love

What is your inner compass set to? Are you aware of having an inner compass at all or are you helplessly buffeted by the wind and weather of emotion, the victim of external forces from the moment your feet touch the ground in the morning to the moment you embrace the dark of night?

Try setting your compass to the true north of love. When your eyes open at daylight do you love what or who you see? Do you love the face on the pillow beside you? If you do, lucky you. If not, why are they in your bed at all?

If you are the only person in your bed, do you love your sheets? The colour of your walls? The objects on your bedside table? The pattern of your curtains or the view from your window? If the answer is no, you might feel a bit depressed. It might be difficult to change the person in your bed or the view from your window but it is not at all difficult to change your curtains or your sheets. Once you start to make a conscious choice and choose things that you love, a profound change can be set in motion.

William Morris said we should not have anything in our homes that we do not find to be useful or believe to be beautiful. Here is my counsel of perfection. Do not have anything in your life that you do not love.

Make love the most over-used word in your vocabulary. Let it kick out routine and habit. When you get dressed in the morning, do you love your underwear, your shoes, your fragrance, your ties, your clothes? Did you buy them because you loved them or because you're stuck wearing a uniform, or because you thought they were cheap or inoffensive or useful and would cover your lumpy bits? Do you love the way they make you feel or do they make you feel comfortably invisible?

Do you love what you eat for breakfast or is it a mindless habit? Do you have an activity you love to look forward to at the end of the day or do you watch television. Do you really love watching television? Do you love your neighbourhood or is it just handy for transport?

You get the idea. Every single waking moment of our lives offers us choices we can exercise through love, and the simpler the choice, the easier it is to make it with love. We can choose to build love from the ground up instead of grasping it out of some future sky.

I love fresh flowers. I love the bunch of daffodils I bought for less than a pound which sits in a blue jug I love on the faded tablecloth I love because I bought it on holiday, spread on the wooden table I love because I fell for the grain and sheen of its surface. This cumulation of simple objects kickstarts my day each morning.

My act of love is the act of attention which takes each object in and acknowledges its place in my life. I can swallow a bowl of cereal inattentively or I can sit at my table and enjoy it slowly, appreciating the blue-rimmed china bowl I eat it from, enjoying the company of my jug of daffodils and the view of the clump of bamboo in my garden which I can see bending in the morning wind. I love the bamboo and the way it dances. I love the fact that I planted it from a pot and it is now a little grove of stems that give me shade in summer.

If there are people at my breakfast table, I can grunt at them from behind the newspaper, which I admit I often do, or I can perform that act of attention, of gratitude, that consciously takes in their presence, listens to what they say, gives thanks for their company. If I have started my day with love I have a small head start on the brutal forces of indifference and chaos that awaits us all. And I have also tuned myself to recognise and experience love in the confusion and variousness of the day ahead. If my inner compass is set to love, I may get lost a thousand times but it will always guide me home.

Everything I've Ever Learned About Love will be available in October 2005. For more information call 020 8962 1230 or visit www.hayhouse.co.uk

HAY HOUSE PUBLISHERS

We hope you enjoyed this Hay House book.
If you would like to receive a free catalogue featuring additional
Hay House books and products, or if you would like information
about the Hay Foundation, please contact:

Hay House UK Ltd

292B Kensal Rd • London W10 5BE
Tel: (44) 20 8962 1230; Fax: (44) 20 8962 1239
www.hayhouse.co.uk

***

Published and distributed in the United States of America by:
Hay House, Inc. • PO Box 5100 • Carlsbad, CA 92018-5100
Tel: (1) 760 431 7695 or (800) 654 5126;
Fax: (1) 760 431 6948 or (800) 650 5115
www.hayhouse.com

Published and distributed in Australia by:
Hay House Australia Ltd • 18/36 Ralph St • Alexandria NSW 2015
Tel: (61) 2 9669 4299 • Fax: (61) 2 9669 4144
www.hayhouse.com.au

Published and distributed in the Republic of South Africa by:
Hay House SA (Pty) Ltd • PO Box 990 • Witkoppen 2068
Tel/Fax: (27) 11 467 8904 • www.hayhouse.co.za

Distributed in Canada by:
Raincoast • 9050 Shaughnessy St • Vancouver, BC V6P 6E5
Tel: (1) 604 323 7100 • Fax: (1) 604 323 2600

***

Sign up via the Hay House UK website to receive the Hay House
online newsletter and stay informed about what's going on with
your favourite authors. You'll receive bimonthly announcements
about discounts and offers, special events, product highlights,
free excerpts, giveaways, and more!
www.hayhouse.co.uk